CONTENTS

Ireland

HARBINGER OF THE MIDDLE AGES

LUDWIG BIELER

LONDON
OXFORD UNIVERSITY PRESS
NEW YORK · TORONTO
1963

Oxford University Press, Amen House, London E.C. 4
GLASGOW NEW YORK TORONTO MELBOURNE WELLINGTON BOMBAY CALCUTTA MADRAS
KARACHI KUALA LUMPUR CAPE TOWN IBADAN NAIROBI ACCRA

PRINTED IN SWITZERLAND

PRINTED BY: WALTER–VERLAG AG OLTEN   BLOCKS BY: F. SCHWITTER AG BASEL

PREFACE

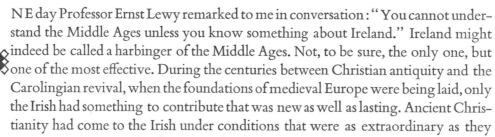

ONE day Professor Ernst Lewy remarked to me in conversation: "You cannot understand the Middle Ages unless you know something about Ireland." Ireland might indeed be called a harbinger of the Middle Ages. Not, to be sure, the only one, but one of the most effective. During the centuries between Christian antiquity and the Carolingian revival, when the foundations of medieval Europe were being laid, only the Irish had something to contribute that was new as well as lasting. Ancient Christianity had come to the Irish under conditions that were as extraordinary as they were unique, and its integration into Ireland's national culture is without parallel. Early Christian Ireland, in turn, has for centuries been unrivalled as a spiritual power in continental Europe. All over Western Christendom the traces of Irish monks and teachers bear witness to their country's historic mission. In the fabric of the medieval world the Irish strain is not the most conspicuous one. It is often too subtle to be easily detected, but it could not be missed even where it is latent. In this book I shall endeavour to make it more fully realized.

Besides the fundamental work by James F. Kenney, *The Sources for the Early History of Ireland* (New York, 1929), the following books have frequently been consulted: Max Manitius, *Geschichte der lateinischen Literatur des Mittelalters*, vol. i (Munich, 1911); E. A. Lowe, *Codices Latini Antiquiores*, vols. i–ix (Oxford, 1934–59); Françoise Henry, *Irish Art in the Early Christian Period* (London, 1940); F. J. E. Raby, *A History of Christian-Latin Poetry*, 2nd edition (Oxford, 1953); Rev. John Ryan, S.J., *Irish Monasticism* (Dublin, 1931); H. Daniel-Rops (Editor), *Le Miracle irlandais* (Paris, 1956); English edition, *The Miracle of Ireland* (Dublin, 1959); Nora K. Chadwick and others, *Studies in the Early British Church* (Cambridge, 1958); Máire and Liam de Paor, *Early Christian Ireland* (London, 1958).

I am greatly indebted also to the learned work of such scholars as Bernhard Bischoff, James Carney, Mario Esposito, P. Corbinian Gindele O.S.B., Père Paul Grosjean S.J., Rev. Aubrey Gwynn S.J., Hans Hennig, Wilhelm Levison, George A. Little, Heinz Löwe, François Masai, Peter Meyer, Carl Nordenfalk, Monsignor Georg Schreiber, and Carl Selmer. In some measure this book is also the result of my own research.

The text of this English edition is not a literal translation of the German original. Not only have I tacitly corrected some inaccuracies and minor errors; I have also slightly contracted or expanded the text in a number of places. Criticism, both printed and unprinted, has been taken carefully into account —with one exception. A German critic regrets my silence as regards the Irish element in the Grail Legend and in other medieval romances. This "omission" is deliberate: I share the view of those scholars who doubt that these legends and romantic stories either originated in Ireland or reached continental Europe through Irish channels.

The sources from which translations have been made and those published English translations which are here reproduced (some with slight changes) are listed at the end of the volume. Omissions in translating have been indicated by a series of dots (...).

The verse translations of Irish and Latin poetry, with the exception of the Cellanus verses (p. 99), are by Professor James Carney of the Institute for Advanced Studies, Dublin; he has also supplied the Note on one of these poems printed on p. 144.

I am greatly obliged to my son, Thomas A. Bieler, without whose pertinent criticism my translation would have been far less readable.

Author and publisher wish to acknowledge their great debt of gratitude to numerous museums, libraries and public bodies for permission to reproduce some of their treasures or to draw on their collections of negatives. They also wish to express their gratitude to those publishers (see p. 145) who have given permission to quote extensively from translations of Latin texts the copyright of which is theirs.

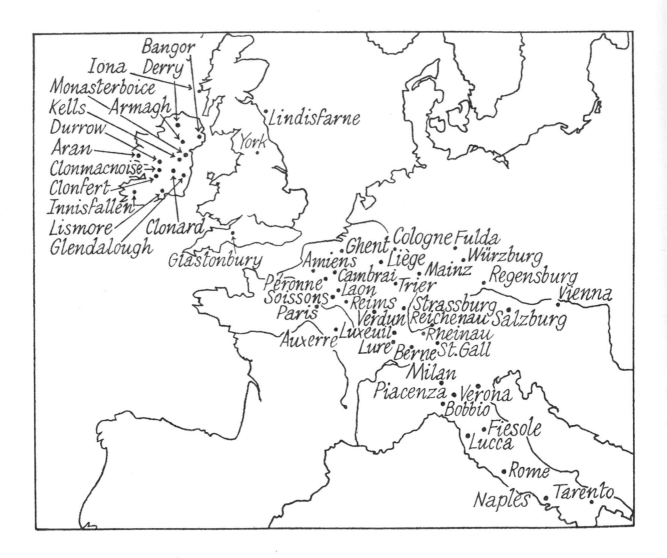

The most important centres of Irish-Christian influence.

IRISH CHRISTIANITY
BEGINNINGS – CHARACTER – EXPANSION

EDIEVAL Europe grew out of the latest phase of Christian antiquity as it developed in the Latin West after the final split in the Roman Empire in the critical years around 400. Many features which to us appear typically medieval have their roots in late antiquity: the *dominatus* of the Christian emperors and feudalism, Teutonic laws and monastic rules, the "arts" as the basic school curriculum and, in the work of Boethius, the beginnings of scholastic method. Roman civilization merged into medieval civilization.

Neither in the intellectual nor in the social sphere was there ever a complete break. Not even the rise of Germanic kingdoms on the soil of the Roman Empire made an essential difference. As soon as the shock of invasion, with all its terrors, was over, the conquerors, or at least their ruling class, made efforts to partake in the higher civilization of their subjects. The Ostrogoths and later the Lombards in Italy, the Franks in Gaul, the Vandals in Africa, but above all the Visigoths in Spain soon joined again the links which had been severed. Even Attila, king of the Huns, surrounded himself with a staff of officers on the Roman model; Orestes, father of the last emperor of the West, had been his secretary. Britain, no longer protected by the Roman legions, fell into a state of political chaos which eventually gave way to the Anglo-Saxon heptarchy. Even there, at least in the thoroughly Romanized south-west, some remnants of Latin learning and Roman civilization stayed alive all through the Dark Ages; allied to national Celtic traditions, this predominantly monastic culture re-asserted itself at a Welsh court as late as the ninth century. A real break occured only when parts of the ancient world —Northern Africa and almost all Spain—fell to Islam.

The age of Charlemagne, on the other hand, regarded classical antiquity, in which it began to take a new interest, as something sufficiently close to itself to serve as a model but at the same time as something distinctly different. It was inevitable that the beginning and end of a process that had gone on for centuries—a process which greatly exceeded the life-span of any individual, and a continuity which would escape the historical comprehension of those times—should appear to a person of the ninth century as essentially different from one another. Even we, who view that process with a highly-developed historical sense and from a considerable distance in time, must admit that a new pattern of life had taken the place of the old one. It is characteristic of the new spirit in which the classics were studied that there was no longer a need to clarify the line of separation from a pagan past as had been necessary for the great writers of ancient Christianity, a Jerome or an Augustine. Classical paganism was dead. In large measure this may have been the inevitable result of the passing of time; but the effect of time would be strengthened and the process accelerated if there existed a Christian culture which was not burdened with such pagan associations. Such a culture did exist—in Ireland, the one and only country to which Christianity had not come in the train of Roman colonization.

In Ireland, the Church would seem to have always been remarkably tolerant towards the pre-Christian native culture. The pagan stories of classical antiquity, which were alien to Ireland's native traditions, would cause even less concern. While giving due prominence to religious learning, the Irish monasteries found room for both native and classical lore. This attitude is reflected in a new form

I

of assimilation; the heritage of pagan as well as Christian antiquity was transformed in a way that made them blend with the traditions of their own past. Together with Irish monasticism and Irish art, this new synthesis was introduced to the Continent by Irish missionaries and teachers. The Germanic tribes that had settled on Roman soil might be expected to have found a similar solution, were it not for the fact that they were engulfed by a world firmly moulded on the Roman pattern; the "barbarians" either remained unaffected, or else became completely absorbed. Continental monasticism, including that of St. Benedict, was indifferent to things of the mind beyond those which bore directly on the spiritual life of the monk; it was not until the middle of the sixth century that Cassiodorus conceived the idea of the monastery as a seat of universal studies, both sacred and profane. In the Irish monasteries, on the other hand, the most important of which were founded in the time of Cassiodorus, learned studies of all kinds seem to have been pursued from the beginning, and apparently were uninfluenced by the Italian scholar.

IRISH ART   Similar is the case of Irish art. Like Celtic and Germanic art in general, it has its roots in the primitive north-western art of pre-historic times, which is in sharp contrast to the classical and post-classical art of the south. As a result of Ireland's political independence of Rome, the influence of Roman provincial art was there only a passing phase. Nor did the Christian missionaries bring late Roman art to Ireland; rather, as might be expected of the archaic monasticism that was introduced into Ireland at an early date, Coptic and Syriac influence had been at work. The several elements, native and foreign, soon combined, and out of their meeting arose an independent national art; the abstract northern style became an artistic expression of Christianity—the first abstract art in the history of Christendom. Although in course of time this art absorbed some Mediterranean elements, it never lost its identity. Its influence can be seen in Carolingian art and in European art of still later times.

 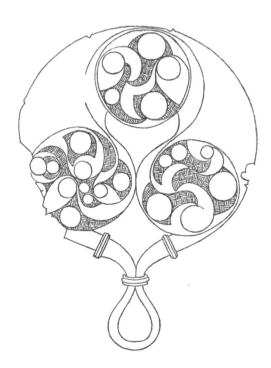

Enamel ornament from a Celtic hanging bowl found in the ship burial of Sutton Hoo, Suffolk. British Museum. – Engraved back of a Celtic bronze mirror in the Mayer Museum, Liverpool. – Opposite: Folio 3 V of the Book of Durrow.

The travels and the settlement of Irish monks and scholars on the Continent of Europe, that complex movement of expansion which, rather summarily, we often call the "Irish Mission", is one of the most important cultural phenomena of the early Middle Ages. There is nothing in pre-Carolingian Europe that could match it in either extent or lasting effect. In Northern France and Burgundy, in the territories of modern Switzerland and Northern Italy, in the Rhine valley, in Franconia, in Bavaria, and in the Salzburg area the *Scotti*, as the Irish were called until the eleventh century, have left their traces. They were as famous for their learning as they were for their religious zeal and for the rigour of their monastic rules; no less well known was their wrangling spirit, which involved them in many a controversy. Even in the Carolingian Empire they played an important role, which was not always to the liking of their continental colleagues.

German writers often refer to the *Scotti peregrini* as "Iro-Schotten". This rather clumsy term is as unnecessary as it is unhistorical. The distinction between Irish and Scottish, which this term implies, did not exist before the eleventh century. Irish emigrants *(Scotti)* colonized the western coast of Caledonia, and later were converted to Christianity by missionaries from their homeland. These *Scotti* gave Scotland her present name. Centuries later the *Scotti* of Scotland began to be distinguished from those of Ireland; the latter were preferably called *Hiberni, Hibernienses,* or *Hibernici.* John Scottus, the great philosopher in the ninth century, was Irish; the schoolman Duns Scotus was Scottish; Petrus Hibernicus, one of the teachers of St. Thomas, and Thomas Hibernicus were Anglo-Irish. The "Schottenmönche" at Ratisbon, Vienna, Erfurt, Würzburg, Nuremberg, and a number of other places were originally Irish; during the later Middle Ages, however, the Irish element gave way more and more to the local one, and eventually these monasteries became continental Benedictine houses. In the early modern period Ratisbon and Würzburg actually counted among their monks a number of Scots; when the Ratisbon "Schottenkloster" was secularized its manuscripts were transported to Scotland (College of Blairs, Aberdeen, and Fort Augustus).

However great was the impression made by Irish saints and scholars who went to the Continent, their art, by and large, did not take root. There is very little in continental architecture, sculpture, mural painting, or ornament on sacred or profane objects that bears witness to their presence. The situation is quite different in the case of book illumination. Irish monks, pilgrims, and teachers took their books with them, and many of these were masterpieces of the illuminator's art. These books and those of their continental disciples—mostly Gospels or Psalters—are among the greatest treasures of secular and ecclesiastical libraries all over Europe. Other manuscripts, less splendidly illuminated, are most valuable to the linguist because of their Irish glosses; from such glosses in manuscripts at Würzburg, Saint Gall, Karlsruhe and Milan the early Irish language was saved from oblivion by Johann Caspar Zeuss (1806–1856). There is no better illustration of the history of the "Irish Mission" than that which is found in the pages of Irish manuscripts.

The Irish mission to the Continent was preceded by a mission to present-day Scotland, and from there to north and east England. A study of this first phase of the expansion of Irish Christianity is essential for our understanding of its subsequent extension to the Continent.

However, we must still go one step further back. When Columcille founded his monastery at Iona and Columbanus crossed to Merovingian Gaul, little more than a century had passed since Ireland herself had first known an organized Christian Church. What prompted the newly converted nation to carry beyond the frontiers of their own country the faith which they had so recently received? An answer, I think, is provided by the very beginnings of Christianity in Ireland.

We do not know when or in what way the Irish first came into contact with Christianity. Commerce with Gaul and the close relations, whether friendly or hostile, with the neighbouring island, whence as early as 314 three bishops were sent to a synod at Arles, offered sufficient opportunities. It has been suggested that Christianity was brought to Ireland by the wine merchants of Burdigala (Bordeaux), who seem to have had an emporium, Bordgal, in Ireland, or, to believe a twelfth-century account (MS Leyden, Vossianus F. 70), by the scholars of Roman Gaul who fled before the Huns and Vandals. More probable mediators would have been the Irish colonies in Britain or individual Irishmen returning from service in the Roman legions. Slowly but steadily the religion of Christian Rome was bound to find its way almost unnoticed to the island on which no Roman legionary had ever set foot.

It is impossible to say how strong the Christian element in Ireland had become by the beginning of the fifth century. Nobody today would believe the legend of St. Mansuetus of Toul according to which this fourth-century (?) bishop was an Irishman and disciple of St. Peter. The famous heretic Pelagius, whose activity falls between the years 384 and 418, is said to have been Irish by birth; it is doubtful, however, whether this can be inferred from St. Jerome's invective against Pelagius in his commentary on Ezekiel. Pelagius' commentary on the Epistles of St. Paul was certainly studied in the Irish schools as late as the ninth century, and Irish expositors of the Bible freely quote their *Pilagius*.

However this may be, there must have been sufficient Christians in Ireland in 431 to justify the Pope sending them a bishop to organize a Church. Under this year a contemporary, the chronicler Prosper of Aquitaine, has the following entry in his annals: "To the Irish believing in Christ Palladius is sent by Pope Celestine as their first bishop." It is tempting to connect this step with another, taken by the same Pope on the suggestion of Palladius—namely the mission to Britain in 429 of the Bishops Germanus and Lupus. This mission also was recorded in Prosper's chronicle. Palladius, who at that time was a deacon of the Church of Rome, was much concerned about the dangers of a revival of Pelagianism in Britain; he might also have contemplated the possible danger of the heresy spreading to the small and scattered Christian communities of Ireland.

Plans for the systematic Christianization of Ireland might very well have been made about that time. A possible reference to such plans is a satirical poem which, as Muirchú informs us in his Life of St. Patrick, was circulated by the druids of Ireland some years before the coming of Patrick. The druids, being the leaders of Irish paganism, would be well aware of such a move.

Adze-head will come,
Across the bold-headed sea,
Hollow-head his mantle,
Bent-head his staff,
His table facing east,
His people, chanting, answer:
Amen, Amen.

The victim of this satire is evidently a foreign bishop, celebrating mass in full *pontificalia*—mitre, chasuble, crozier. It need not be Patrick; but the druids knew what was on the way.

Of Palladius nothing further is heard; another remark of Prosper's (this time in his tract against Cassian, *Contra Collatorem* II.1, a eulogy on the recently deceased Pope Celestine) seems to imply that Palladius had successfully carried out his task. Irish tradition, on the other hand, is reticent as far as Palladius is concerned. He figures only in the legend of St. Patrick, and there he is introduced merely as the dark contrast to the bright figure of the national apostle. Palladius, it is said, founded three churches in Co. Wicklow, but, dissatisfied with the little progress he was able to make, turned his back on

Ireland and died on his return to Rome. According to another version he died as a martyr. On receiving the news of his death, Patrick is ordained bishop, and his preaching has an immediate success. For it is Patrick, and not Palladius, to whom Ireland was given by the Lord. The bias of the seventh-century hagiographer is obvious. All the same, his account need not be entirely rejected. The task of Palladius might have been limited in place and time. He might have come not as a missionary but merely as an organizer; having accomplished what he had come to do, he would, naturally, return. However, even if this were the case, it is easy to understand that this was not the type of person whom the Irish people would remember as their "apostle". This title of honour was given to a Briton, who, against all possible odds, trusted in his divine vocation and gave himself to the work to which he knew himself to be called. This man was St. Patrick.

PATRICK   The vast amount of literature about St. Patrick, of whom so little is known from his own writings and from those of his contemporaries, must be surprising to anyone who has not studied the evidence. Those who have read his *Confession* will understand why this is so. Patrick writes for readers who know what he is talking about. The details of his life and work which he mentions, or to which more often he vaguely alludes, are related because of their spiritual significance and with a view to his self-justification. The Patrick legend, on the other hand, which appears in a literary form after the middle of the seventh century, is closely linked up with the ecclesiastical policy of the "heirs", i.e. the successors, of Patrick, the bishops and abbots of Armagh in Northern Ireland, who aimed at uniting under their jurisdiction all churches which claimed St. Patrick as their founder. A wide field is thus open to the speculation of historians. Most problems seemed to have been solved by the great historian J. B. Bury (*The Life of St. Patrick and His Place in History*, 1905); as a result of more recent research, however, Bury's "solution" has become problematical. The question turns mainly on details of chronology and on principles of historical criticism. For our present purpose we can leave these problems alone, and concentrate on the personality of Ireland's apostle as revealed in his work and in the small body of writings which he left us.

According to the earliest annalistic evidence, which probably dates as far back as the seventh century, Patrick, succeeding Palladius, came to Ireland in 432 and died in 461 or 492/3. Since Bury, most scholars—until recently—have accepted the earlier date of Patrick's death and, by a combination of several details in the *Confession*, have calculated his birthdate at c. 385. Patrick himself tells us that he was the son of a Christian *decurio* (alderman) in some city of Roman Britain. The city is not named, but Patrick says that his father Calpornius had a country estate near that city, at a place called, in the manuscripts, *Bannauem Taberniae* (or *Taburniae*); if Père Grosjean is right in reading this as *Clannauenta Berniciae*, Patrick's birthplace would be Ravenglass in Cumberland, on the west coast of Britain, south of the Clyde. During a temporary sojourn on that estate young Patrick fell into the hands of Irish pirates, at whose mercy the country had been since the retreat of the Roman legions. But let us hear Patrick's own words.

I am Patrick, a sinner, most unlearned, the least of all the faithful, and utterly despised by many. My father was Calpornius, a deacon, son of Potitus, a priest, of the village Bannavem Taberniae (Taburniae); he had a country seat nearby, and there I was taken captive.

I was then about sixteen years of age. I did not know the true God. I was taken into captivity to Ireland with many thousands of people—and deservedly so, because we turned away from God, and did not keep His commandments, and did not obey our priests, who used to remind us of our salvation. And the Lord brought over us the wrath of His anger, and scattered us among many nations, even unto the utmost part of the earth, where now my littleness is placed among strangers.

6

Other details of that raid are mentioned in Patrick's letter to the Welsh prince Coroticus (Ceredig) and his soldiers:

Did I come to Ireland without God, or according to the flesh? Who compelled me? I am bound by the Spirit not to see any of my kinsfolk. Is it of my own doing that I have holy mercy on the people who once took me captive and made away with the servants and maids of my father's house? I was freeborn according to the flesh. I am the son of a decurion. But I sold my noble rank—I am neither ashamed nor sorry—for the good of others. Thus I am a servant in Christ to a foreign nation for the unspeakable glory of life everlasting which is in Christ Jesus our Lord.

There is no contradiction in the fact that Patrick says in one place that his father was a decurion and in another that he was a deacon. Probably Calpornius had taken holy orders in later years—a thing by no means rare in those days. It might have been for him the only way of avoiding the financial burden of his honorary position as alderman; this too would not have been unique in his time.

In his *Confession* Patrick goes on to describe the effect which his Irish captivity had on his mind and the results which his "retreat into himself" produced.

And there the Lord opened the sense of my unbelief that I might at last remember my sins and be converted with all my heart to the Lord my God, who had regard for my abjection, and mercy on my youth and ignorance, and watched over me before I knew Him, and before I was able to distinguish between good and evil, and guarded me, and comforted me as would a father his son....

For this reason I long had in mind to write, but hesitated until now; I was afraid of exposing myself to the talk of men, because I have not studied like the others, who thoroughly imbibed law and Sacred Scripture, and never had to change from the language of their childhood days, but were able to make it still more perfect....

As a youth, nay, almost as a boy not able to speak, I was taken captive, before I knew what to pursue and what to avoid. Hence today I blush and fear exceedingly to reveal my lack of education; for I am unable to tell my story to those versed in the art of concise writing—in such a way, I mean, as my spirit and mind long to do, and so that the sense of my words expresses what I feel....

Whence I, once rustic, exiled, unlearned, who does not know how to provide for the future, this at least I know most certainly that before I was humiliated I was like a stone lying in the deep mire; and He that is mighty came and in His mercy lifted me up, and raised me aloft, and placed me on the top of the wall. And therefore I ought to cry out aloud and so also render something to the Lord for His great benefits here and in eternity—benefits which the mind of men is unable to appraise.

Wherefore, then, be astonished, ye great and little that fear God, and you men of letters on your estates, listen and pore over this. Who was it that roused up me, the fool that I am, from the midst of those who in the eyes of men are wise, and expert in law, and powerful in word and in everything? And He inspired me—me, the outcast of this world—before others, to be the man (if only I could!) who, with fear and reverence and without blame, should faithfully serve the people to whom the love of Christ conveyed and gave me for the duration of my life, if I should be worthy; yes indeed, to serve them humbly and sincerely....

And I was not worthy, nor was I such that the Lord should grant this to His servant; that after my misfortunes and so great difficulties, after my captivity, after the lapse of so many years, He should give me so great a grace in behalf of that nation—a thing which once, in my youth, I never expected nor thought of.

But after I came to Ireland—every day I had to tend sheep, and many times a day I prayed—the love of God and His fear came to me more and more, and my faith was strengthened. And my spirit was moved so that in a single day I would say as many as a hundred prayers, and almost as many in the night, and this even when I was staying in the woods and on the mountain; and I used to get up for prayer before daylight, through snow, through frost, through rain, and I felt no harm, and there was no sloth in me—as I now see, because the spirit within me was then fervent.

And there one night I heard in my sleep a voice saying to me: "It is well that you fast, soon you will go to your own country." And again, after a short while, I heard a voice saying to me: "See, your ship is ready." And it was not near, but at a distance of perhaps two hundred miles, and I had never been there, nor did I know a living soul there; and then I took to flight, and I left the man with whom I had stayed for six years. And I went in the strength of God who directed my way to my good, and I feared nothing until I came to that ship.

And the day that I arrived the ship was set afloat, and I said that I was able to pay for my passage with them. But the captain was not pleased, and with indignation he answered harshly: "It is of no use for you to ask us to go along with us." And when I heard this, I left them in order to return to the hut where I was staying. And as I went, I began to pray; and before I had ended my prayer, I heard one of them shouting behind me: "Come, hurry, we shall take you on in good faith; make friends with us in whatever way you like." And so on that day I refused to suck their breasts for fear of God, but rather hoped they would come to the faith of Jesus Christ, because they were pagans. And thus I had my way with them, and we set sail at once.

And after three days we reached land, and for twenty-eight days we travelled through deserted country. And they lacked food, and hunger overcame them; and the next day the captain said to me: "Tell me, Christian: you say that your God is great and all-powerful; why, then, do you not pray for us? As you can see, we are suffering from hunger; it is unlikely indeed that we shall ever see a human being again."

I said to them full of confidence: "Be truly converted with all your heart to the Lord my God, because nothing is impossible for Him, that this day He may send you food on your way until you be satisfied; for He has abundance everywhere." And, with the help of God, so it came to pass: suddenly a herd of pigs appeared on the road before our eyes, and they killed many of them; and there they stopped for two nights and fully recovered their strength, and their hounds received their fill, for many of them had grown weak and were half-dead along the way. And from that day they had plenty of food. They also found wild honey, and offered some of it to me, and one of them said: "This we offer in sacrifice." Thanks be to God, I tasted none of it.

That same night, when I was asleep, Satan assailed me violently, a thing I shall remember as long as I shall be in this body. And he fell upon me like a huge rock, and I could not stir a limb. But whence came it into my mind, ignorant as I am, to call upon Helias? And meanwhile I saw the sun rise in the sky, and while I was shouting "Helias! Helias!" with all my might, suddenly the splendour of that sun fell on me and immediately freed me of all misery. And I believe that I was sustained by Christ my Lord, and that His Spirit was even then crying out in my behalf....

And once again, after many years, I fell into captivity. On that first night I stayed with them. I heard a divine message saying to me: "Two months will you be with them." And so it came to pass: on the sixtieth night thereafter the Lord delivered me out of their hands.

Also on our way God gave us food and fire and dry weather every day, until, on the tenth day, we met people. As I said above, we travelled twenty-eight days through deserted country, and the night that we met people we had no food left.

And again after a few years I was in Britain with my people, who received me as their son, and sincerely besought me that now at last, having suffered so many hardships, I should not leave them and go elsewhere.

And there I saw in the night the vision of a man, whose name was Victoricus, coming as it were from Ireland, with countless letters. And he gave me one of them, and I read the opening words of the letter, which were, "The voice of the Irish"; and as I read the beginning of the letter I thought that at the same moment I heard their voice—they were those beside the Wood of Voclut, which is near the Western Sea—and thus did they cry out as with one mouth: "We ask thee, boy, come and walk among us once more."

And I was quite broken in heart, and could read no further, and so I woke up. Thanks be to God, after many years the Lord gave to them according to their cry.

And another night—whether within me, or beside me, I know not, God knoweth—they called me most un-mistakably with words which I heard but could not understand, except that at the end of the prayer He spoke thus: "He that has laid down His life for thee, it is that speaketh in thee"; and so I awoke full of joy.

And again I saw Him praying in me, and I was as it were within my body, and I heard Him above me, that is, over the inward man, and there he prayed mightily with groanings. And all the time I was astonished, and wondered, and thought with myself who it could be that prayed in me. But at the end of the prayer He spoke, saying that He was the Spirit; and so I woke up, and remembered the Apostle saying: The Spirit helpeth the infirmities of our prayer. For we know not what we should pray for as we ought; but the Spirit Himself asketh for us with unspeakable groanings, which cannot be expressed in words; and again: The Lord our advocate asketh for us.

Patrick does not tell us where he received his ecclesiastical training. His seventh-century Irish biographers quote a "Saying" of his which gives at least a hint.

"The fear of God I had as my guide on my way through Gaul and Italy and the islands of the Tyrrhene Sea."

Late in life, he still feels a desire to go to Gaul and to visit there "the saints of the Lord" (*Confession*, § 43). The Lives represent him as a disciple of St. Germanus of Auxerre (bishop 418–c. 448), which may be taken as historically accurate; that he should have had personal relations with St. Martin of Tours is, however, unbelievable on grounds of chronology. It is quite certain that Patrick got to know monasticism in its primitive form. Monasticism was then a new thing in the West, and spread mainly among the islands of the Tyrrhene Sea, which are mentioned in Patrick's *dictum*. A tradition which makes St. Patrick a disciple of St. Honoratus at Lérins, though still alive to this day, cannot be substantiated. Patrick brought this archaic, pre-Benedictine monasticism to Ireland; there it flourished for many generations until, in the twelfth century, the continental orders, and in particular the Cistercians, were brought over from France, and later from England. The growth of monasticism was counted by Patrick as one of the finest fruits of his missionary work. Monasticism was then the latest, the most up-to-date development of Christian life, and Patrick at once transplanted the new shoot to the "Church of the Irish". Twice in his writings he says, with almost the same words: "The sons of the Irish and the daughters of their kings are monks and brides of Christ." And he tells the story of a noble Irishwoman who, shortly after baptism, took the veil in obedience to a divine message.

With all his love for his new converts, which speaks to us so intensely in his letter against the raider Coroticus, and with all his "glorying in Christ" as he looks back at the fruits of his labours, Patrick remained a "Roman" at heart to the end of his days. He felt himself a citizen of the Roman Empire, though a Roman in exile. His life in Ireland was for him a "second captivity" after the first one in his youth; but it was a "captivity in the Spirit", from which he dared not escape:

Even if I wished to leave them (the Irish) and to go to Britain, to my country and my people, and also to Gaul in order to visit the brethren and to see the face of the saints of my Lord—God knows how much I desired it—I am bound by the Spirit, who gives evidence against me if I do this, telling me that I shall be guilty; and I am afraid of losing the labour which I have begun—nay, not I, but Christ the Lord who bade me come here and stay with them for the rest of my life, if the Lord will.

Here speaks the missionary who for the sake of God has left his country for good, who has chosen voluntary exile, sacrificing himself for the salvation of others. Is this not the prototype of the Irish missionary?

However, the "Irish Mission" is too complex a phenomenon to be explained by a single motive.

Not always, and not necessarily in the first place, did the Irish leave their country with the intention of becoming missionaries in foreign parts. Many of them went to countries which for a long time past had been Christian at least in name. In France and Northern Italy they would most certainly encounter laxity, heresy, and in the countryside even remnants of paganism. A wide field for apostolic work awaited them everywhere, and they did not fail to take up the challenge by their teaching and by their example. This is as true of Dungal and John Scottus in the middle of the ninth century as it was of Columbanus at the turn of the sixth. But the Irish monks went into voluntary exile first and foremost with the intention of leading the "perfect life". Complete renunciation of the world and a most rigorous form of asceticism were practised even by those Irish and British monks who stayed at home; to this the *peregrini* added the special sacrifice of leaving their country for the remainder of their lives, which according to Irish secular law was a punishment for very grave crimes. The Irish Church kept to the Old Testament more closely than did the Church on the Continent; this can be seen, for example, in their observance of the Mosaic Law concerning clean and unclean food. Similarly, God's command to Abraham: "Go forth from thy country, from thy kin and thy family, to the country that I shall show thee" (Genesis xii.1) was understood by many as a call to perfection that ought to be obeyed to the letter.

Another motive, however, was almost equally strong—the *Wanderlust*, inherent in the Irish, which then as now would urge them to leave their island for far-off lands. The raiding bands of the *fianna*, adventurous heroes like Froich, far-travelled sailors like Maelduin come to mind as counterparts of these Christian "wanderers", while in the legendary voyage of St. Brendan and his companions—some scholars believe that he discovered Florida as early as the sixth century—we actually possess the Christian parallel of a mythical sea-voyage. The *Navigatio Sancti Brendani*, with its fantastic stories, which have parallels in the Tales of Sindbad, was one of the most beloved books of the Middle Ages; it was still popular in the times of Columbus and gave him a stimulus to his own discoveries.

A further motive was the attraction of ecclesiastical and secular centres abroad where learning and learned poetry were welcomed. In the ninth century the Carolingian Empire experienced a regular "invasion" by scholars and poets from Ireland. For the greater part these were neither monks nor priests; they were, in all probability, clerics. At a time when in their own country intellectual culture declined more and more under the impact of frequent raids by the Norsemen, the revival of learning on the Continent, which had just then begun, must have had a tremendous appeal for these savants. In the circumstances it seems pardonable enough if some of them blew their trumpets rather loudly. They may not all have been as good as their word; but many of them were well able to hold their own with their Italian, Spanish, and Anglo-Saxon colleagues. Their contribution to Carolingian culture is far from insignificant, and they had their fair share in Charlemagne's great work of education. One of these scholars, John Eriugena ("scion of Eire") was to become the one and only speculative theologian and philosopher of this time—a lone figure in the intellectual history of the early Middle Ages.

Renunciation of one's country for the love of God (the Abraham and Patrick motive), missionary zeal, *Wanderlust*, the raids of the Scandinavians, and since the time of the Carolingians also the attraction of foreign cultural centres—these, in varying strength, were the stimuli behind the "Irish Mission". There was another less demonstrable motive, that of a quarrel at home and the emigration of the defeated party. Bede (*Ecclesiastical History*, iv.4) tells us that the Irish bishop Colmán of Lindisfarne, after his defeat at Whitby, retired with his Irish monks first to Iona, whence he had come, and later to the West of Ireland. Of an exodus in the opposite direction only one instance is on record, and this is legendary—the emigration of St. Columba from Ireland to Scotland. Our earliest and most reliable authority, Adamnán of Iona, who wrote a Life of St. Columba less than a hundred years after the saint's death, knows nothing of a dispute which caused his exile. Adamnán merely says that Columba left Ireland because he wished to be an exile for Christ; he was possibly the first among the Irish to do so. A *Life of St. Columba*, however, in the late medieval collection of Codex Insulensis (Oxford, Bodleian Library, Rawlinson B 485) and the Irish *Life of Columcille* which was compiled in 1532 by order of Manus O'Donnell contain a long and interesting story about the cause of Columba's exile. One day Columba visited Finnian of Druim Finn. His host lent him a book—the O'Donnell Life has it that this was the famous Psalter which later became the battle talisman *(cathach)* of the O'Donnells—and Columba, a great lover of books, copied it secretly at night in Finnian's church. However, Finnian found him out and objected strongly to Columba's behaviour. They eventually agreed to bring their dispute before the king, Diarmait mac Cerr-béil. Finnian accused Columba of having taken a copy of his book without his permission; Columba claimed that Finnian's book had lost non of its value for having been copied, and even suggested that it was not right to put obstacles in the way of copying a sacred text and thus making it more widely known. The issue, however, was firmly decided by Diarmait: "As the calf follows the cow, so the copy follows the original." Far from accepting the king's verdict, Columba cursed Diarmait and walked out in anger. The king then prepared for war against Columba's people. When the parties joined battle at Cul Dremhne, Columba obtained victory for his side by prayer and fasting; an angel in the shape of a giant soldier walked in front of them and so frightened the enemy that three thousand of them lost their lives. For that victory the angel demanded that Columba pay with the sacrifice of permanent exile. According to another version, Columba had scruples about the bloodshed which he had caused, and consulted another saint about a suitable penance. The latter told him to leave his country for ever and to win as many souls for God as men killed in the battle. Opinions are divided as to whether this story contains even a shred of historical truth. Columba's eagerness to copy books is well attested quite apart from this story; so is Finnian's jealousy with regard to his own library. The *Cathach*, one of the earliest copies of the "Gallican Psalter", and the only one known to have existed in early Ireland, must certainly have been a book which Finnian would have guarded most jealously, and which Columba would have been most anxious to copy; but the detail that their quarrel started over this book belongs only to the latest form in which this legend is known.

Lines with initial from the *Cathach* of St. Columba.

The Irish abroad were not only a leaven in religious life, they were at the same time agents who transmitted, or rather re-introduced, some of the culture of classical antiquity that had been lost or had vanished out of sight on the Continent. Columbanus showed a remarkable familiarity with Latin poets from the Augustan period to his own time; Virgil of Salzburg aroused the suspicion of St. Boniface because, on the authority of ancient sources, he taught the existence of antipodes. Dicuil displayed a competent knowledge of ancient astronomy and geography; Sedulius Scottus was not only a Biblical scholar who studied bilingual texts of the sacred books; he was also the first for centuries to study—and to imitate—Horace. When the Irish abbot Cellanus of Péronne in Picardy (c. 700) composed an epigram in honour of St. Patrick, he modelled it deliberately on the epitaph of Virgil (*Mantua me genuit...*). Towering above all the others, John Eriugena gives proof not only of a surprisingly good knowledge of the Greek language, but—what is more surprising in his time—of a profound and extensive study of Christian Neo-Platonists. Not only does he know their writings, he thinks independently along the same lines. The classicism of these men contrasts sharply with the spirit of the pioneers of Irish Christianity.

Compared to his contemporaries, Patrick was uneducated, and he knew it. Those who had opposed his appointment as bishop for Ireland went on harping on his "rusticity" even after many years of a most successful mission:

Many tried to prevent this my mission; they would even talk to one another behind my back and say: "Why does this fellow throw himself into danger among enemies who have no knowledge of God?" It was not malice, but it did not appeal to them because—and to this I own myself—of my rusticity.

The earliest Latin poem written in Ireland—the hymn in honour of St. Patrick which is attributed to Bishop Secundinus (d. 447)—stems in form and style from popular Christian verse; it is in many ways similar to Augustine's *Psalmus contra Partem Donati*, the battle-song of the orthodox against the heretic Donatus, which might in actual fact have been its model. The hymn is rich in Biblical reminiscences; there is in it not a trace of classical Latin poetry. Little more than a century later Columbanus, according to his biographer Jonas of Bobbio, devoted himself from early childhood to grammatical and literary studies (*Life of St. Columbanus*, i.3). How is this change to be explained?

It is not only this interest in classical antiquity which sets the Irish Church of the sixth century apart from that of the fifth, but also a change in its organization. For all his love of monasticism, Patrick did not organize his missionary church on monastic lines, but on the continental pattern, in parishes and dioceses (both were at that time called *paruchia*), under priests and bishops respectively. From the canons of a synod, issued with the approval of Patrick and his fellow bishops Auxilius and Iserninus, probably in 457, we see quite clearly that the bishop was to have absolute jurisdiction in his diocese. By the end of the sixth century, on the other hand, the centres of ecclesiastical life were to be found in the monasteries, especially in the powerful associations (*familiae*) of monasteries which had the same founder. Their abbots were the princes of the Irish Church. The bishops gained high respect because of their powers of ordination and often because of their piety and learning; but they had no authority. The *Catalogus Sanctorum Hiberniae*, which dates from the ninth or tenth century, says that the saints of the first order (Patrick, his contemporaries and disciples) were almost all bishops, whereas the saints of the second order (the founders of the great monasteries in the sixth century) were for the greater part priests.

These priests had received their liturgies from the saints in Wales, from David, Gildas, and Docco. This is by no means the only source that refers to, or suggests, some influence of the Welsh Church on the Irish Church. It seems quite feasible that the sudden interest in Latin learning also came this way. Unfortunately we know even less about the Church in Wales in the sixth century than we know about the Church in Ireland. The lives of Welsh saints—except the oldest Life of St. Samson, who emigrated to Brittany and founded Dol—were written during the eleventh and twelfth centuries for the purpose of proving to the Anglo-Norman conquerors the antiquity and the importance of the Welsh sees. It is uncertain what elements of genuine tradition they contain. It is arguable, however, that in Wales longer than elsewhere in Britain some remnants of Roman intellectual culture survived the retreat of the Roman legions.

At this point it is necessary to say something about a very strange piece of literature (if it may be so called) which apparently influenced some British as well as some Irish authors (Gildas, Columba, Adamnán, and others)—the *Hisperica Famina*. Even its title, which hardly means more than "Latin Composition", gives an idea of its style. It is in an obscure and artificial Latin idiom, which deliberately avoids all ordinary forms of expression. The greatest obstacle to its understanding is its vocabulary, largely "gloss Latin". That is to say that a great number of "Hisperic" words are found in glossaries, in lists of rare and difficult words culled either from the Latin poets or from the Bible. Such a "superliterary" language is typical of a period of decline or even decay; it can be understood as the reaction of a learned clique to the progressive disintegration of classical Latin. However, the style of the "Hisperic" authors (or author) is as far removed from the classical "mean" as is that of the writers of Vulgar Latin. Where and when the *Hisperica Famina* were composed is a much discussed problem. Everything points to the western islands, either Britain or Ireland, and to the sixth or seventh century. To decide between the claims of Wales and Ireland is difficult; recently one of the best scholars in this field, Père P. Grosjean, has strongly pleaded for Ireland. It might all have started with a single person, who obviously came from abroad, whether from Gaul, or from Spain, or from Wales —who knows? Similar productions, but with a different vocabulary, are occasionally found elsewhere: for example, in one of the prose prefaces of the Latin Anthology, which was compiled in Africa. This laboured idiom was not only imitated in Ireland by writers of Latin, but has its counterpart also in Gaelic. The Irish word for it is *retoric*, and the foreign term is suggestive of a foreign model.

The character and extent of classical education in early Ireland is as much a matter of speculation as is its origin. We know quite a number of Irish "classicists" on the Continent. The crucial question is: how much of their classical learning did they acquire at home? Unfortunately, there is no clear and unequivocal answer. One thing is certain, however: the Irish did not have a classical education in the modern meaning of the term. The knowledge of classical authors, both poets and prose writers, which some Irishmen on the Continent—Columbanus, Donatus of Fiesole, Sedulius Scottus—displayed need not necessarily have been acquired entirely at home. The fact that Horace, whose works had been almost forgotten for two hundred years, is revived in ninth-century France, and invariably in an Irish milieu, proves nothing more than that the Irish—as anyone who knows them will understand—felt attracted by his poetry and brought it to light wherever they found it. The literary interests of the Irish who stayed at home, as well as those of them who evangelized Scotland and, later, Northumbria, hardly go beyond that which we expect to encounter in the late Latin period. On the whole they are confined to ecclesiastical writings, textbooks of the arts, and a minimum of classroom authors. Apart from these, the Irish knew such Christian poets as Juvencus and Sedulius, and occasionally a work that had become rare on the Continent, for example the *Chronicle* of Sulpicius Severus. Sixth-century Ireland has no Boethius or Cassiodorus, no Venantius Fortunatus, no Isidore. Nevertheless, wherever they went, the Irish were surrounded by an aura of superior learning: Aldhelm and Bede in Anglo-Saxon England, the *Casus Sancti Galli* and Heiric of Auxerre in Carolingian France bear witness to this reputation. Only Theodulf of Orléans does not hide his contempt for the strange and, to him, abstruse erudition of the Irishman Cadac. The Irish who went to the Continent must have learnt a great deal that was new to them; in particular, they would become acquainted with the manuscripts of classical authors that had never reached their shores. The seed, however, that multiplied in the new soil had come from home.

Much the same is true of Ireland's role in the transmission of Greek. Few problems in this field of literary history have been discussed as often and debated as hotly as this one. There is no evidence whatsoever to show that the ancient Irish knew even a single writer or poet of classical Greece in the original. Some works of the Greek Fathers which were little known, or even unknown, in the West seem to have reached Ireland in translation. It is possible, and certainly arguable, that in some places a scholar could get elementary instruction in Greek grammar. There seem also to have existed in Ireland some Graeco-Latin glossaries and conversation-books. Many Irish scribes were familiar with the Greek alphabet and used it as a specially solemn script; for example, the Lord's Prayer in the Book of Armagh (c. 807) is written in Greek letters, although the text is in Latin. They wanted to have some knowledge of Greek, even if they were unable to write it, just as they affected a knowledge of Hebrew. Hebrew, Greek, and Latin were the three "sacred languages", the languages of the title on the cross of Christ. Adamnán renders the name of St. Columcille as Jona, Peristera, Columba ("dove" in the three languages respectively), and St. Columbanus in some of his letters renders his own name likewise. This a practice well known from Irish commentaries on the Bible. The expositor is always at pains to give the name of a person, a place, or anything of importance in the three "sacred languages". We are not altogether surprised to find in these commentaries some rather spurious Greek and even more spurious Hebrew. To give just one example: Irish Biblical expositors are responsible for the fact that the unnamed and unnumbered magi from the East who came to adore the newly born Christ became, in western legend, the three holy kings, Caspar, Melchior, and Balthasar. Among the several "trilingual" sets of names of the magi in the Irish commentaries on St. Matthew we find Melchio, Aspar, Patisara. Apart from such incursions into bogus Greek and Hebrew, the Irish did their best to get as much out of the sources at their disposal as they possibly could. They were well acquainted with the *Interpretatio Nominum Hebraicorum* of St. Jerome, and they so industriously culled the Greek words used by the Latin Fathers that generations of modern scholars jumped to the conclusion that they must have had a first-hand knowledge of Greek. It is on the Continent once again that these studies came to full fruition. Sedulius Scottus studied and copied Graeco-Latin bilingual manuscripts, and a man of genius such as John Eriugena not only worked his way through the Pseudo-Areopagite and translated him but also studied such Greek theologians as Maximus Confessor; he even attempted to write Greek verse. It has been suggested that John might have had contacts with Greek monks in either Southern France or Italy. Opportunities for such contacts did exist, but there is no evidence to show that John had any.

It is more than likely that the Irish made an original contribution to medieval Latin poetry which was to be of the greatest importance in the future, namely the rhyme as a formal element of verse. Ancient poetry knew only metres, that is to say, lines the structure of which was determined by a regular sequence of long and short syllables. Rhyme was a constituent of formal prose, not of poetry; and where it is found in a poem, as often in the hexameter of Ovid, it is a mannerism, a trespassing of rhetoric into poetry. When, in the phonetic development of late Latin, the feeling for ancient prosody was lost, metrical versification would have come to an end had it not been cultivated artifically in learned circles and eventually handed down to the schools of the Middle Ages. Popular verse in late

Latin is different: it is based either on a mere count of syllables or on the stress accent of the spoken language. A poem of this type is found among the earliest Latin hymns of the Irish Church—the hymn of St. Secundinus on Patrick. The earliest manuscript in which this poem is preserved, the Antiphonary of Bangor, which was written at the end of the seventh century, contains, however, also a poem of a very different type—the verses on the community *(munther)* of Bangor. This poem, half Irish, half Latin, in accentuating lines, makes use of the rhyme:

navis nunquam turbata

quamvis fluctibus tonsa,

nuptis quoque parata

regi domino sponsa.

Other rhyming poems are the *De Mundi Transitu* (on the passing away of earthly things) by St. Columbanus, and the hymn *Altus Prosator* ascribed to St. Columcille. That this is something specifically Irish is suggested also by the character of the native poetry of Ireland, which, in contrast to the initial rhyme ("Stabreim") of Germanic poetry, has developed an elaborate system of end-rhyme and even internal rhyme.

However large or small a sector of classical learning was covered in the Irish schools, there can be no doubt that Irish scholars strove most earnestly and assiduously to assimilate to the full what was at their disposal, and to make it completely their own. For many generations the Irish had had a national culture which was handed down orally, and Irish society included a well organized class of poets and scholars who enjoyed a high social reputation. Irish national learning also came under the influence of Latin learning, but this process lies outside our subject. It was perfectly natural that the Irish, having become Christians, should be as appreciative of the new learning as they had been of their own traditional lore. This attitude is characteristic of Irish monasticism. The essential difference between the two types of learning is the important role of the written as well as the oral tradition in the monastic schools. *Sapiens*, "the wise man", and *scriba*, which does not only mean "scribe" (a copyist of texts) but normally designates the head of a monastic school (including its scriptorium) and thence comes to mean "man of letters", are titles of honour which the Annals give to a number of monks, abbots, and bishops. The great respect which the Irish had for the written word and its transmission is manifested most impressively by the fact that they developed a style of handwriting all their own, a national script.

Of all the numerous types of Latin script which came into existence during the early Middle Ages, the Irish script has had the longest life and the widest dissemination. All the other ancient "national scripts" of Europe had to give way to the superior qualities of clarity and practicability of the Carolingian minuscule (the model of the script of the humanists, and through them of our Roman printing type); only the Irish script continued to be practised at home until the Anglo-Norman invasion of the twelfth century. Even when, with the conquerors and the continental religious orders, late romanesque and gothic hands had come into use, the ancient Irish script continued to be employed for the writing of texts in the Irish language, and is so employed to the present day. In earlier times this script travelled as far as did the *Scotti peregrini*. From Iona it was imported to Northumbria. The stylistic variety which developed there, and which we call Anglo-Saxon, narrower, more jejune and more regular in appearance, soon conquered the whole of Anglo-Saxon England. Like its model in Ireland,

IRISH SCRIPT

it survived the reception of continental minuscule and the Norman Conquest as a means of recording texts in the national language; the only change required was the addition of some runic letters to represent the sounds peculiar to Anglo-Saxon. On the Continent, the Irish script never had such a strong position as it had in pre-Conquest England. The Irish and Anglo-Saxon scholars who crossed the Channel continued to write the script which they had learnt at home; this is proved by manuscripts in "insular" hands written abroad, such as the Salzburg Cuthbercht Gospels (now in Vienna, National Library, Lat. 1224), or, as late as the end of the eleventh century, the autograph chronicle of Marianus Scottus (Vatican, Palatinus lat. 830). However, in a foreign milieu with its own writing traditions the insular types of script, which continental scholars found difficult to read, were never preserved unaltered for more than a generation. Before long we witness the development of mixed styles (which can best be studied in the Bobbio scriptorium), and in the end they, along with the genuine continental scripts, are ousted by the victorious Carolingian minuscule. The insular element, however, clearly recognizable to the palaeographer's eye, asserted itself throughout the ninth century, and even later, in many ways in the ductus, in ligatures, and especially in the presence of characteristic insular abbreviations. The latter became so generally accepted that from the scholastic period onwards they were employed universally, and quite independently of Irish or Anglo-Saxon influence.

Irish majuscule, Book of Durrow, 7th century.

Irish majuscule, Codex 51 of the Stiftsbibliothek of St. Gall, 8th–9th century.

Irish minuscule in the St. Gall MS of Priscian's Grammar (c. 850).

Carolingian minuscule, second half of the 9th century.

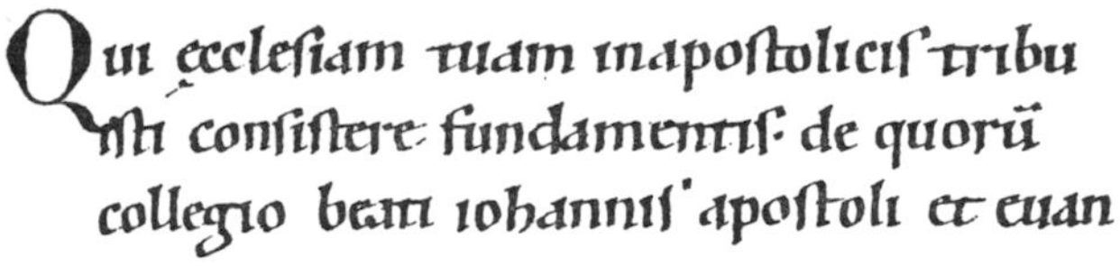

Qui ecclesiam tuam inapostolicis tribu
ñh consistere fundamentis de quorū
collegio beati iohannis apostoli et euan

Carolingian minuscule, 11th century.

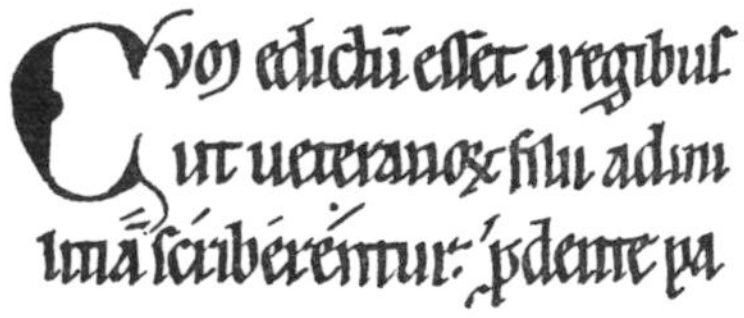

Cvor edictū esset aregibus
ut ueteranorū filii admi
litia scriberentur: idente pa

Carolingian pre-Gothic minuscule, 12th century.

The significance of the Irish script as a cultural symptom emerges most clearly when its genesis is compared with that of the other "national scripts" of the early Middle Ages. All the others—the Visigothic script in Spain, the Beneventan script in Southern Italy, the local types of the Merovingian kingdom, the Rhaetian and Alemannic scripts in the districts of Chur and Saint Gall, and the less characteristic scripts of Northern Italy and Western Germany—can be understood as attempts at normalizing the degenerate cursive script of late antiquity in the hope of thus producing a serviceable book-hand. The Irish script, it seems, was a deliberate creation out of elements of the several scripts inherited from antiquity which the earliest missionaries had brought with them. That this was the case is suggested by the fact that Irish scribes from early times employ two distinct types of script side

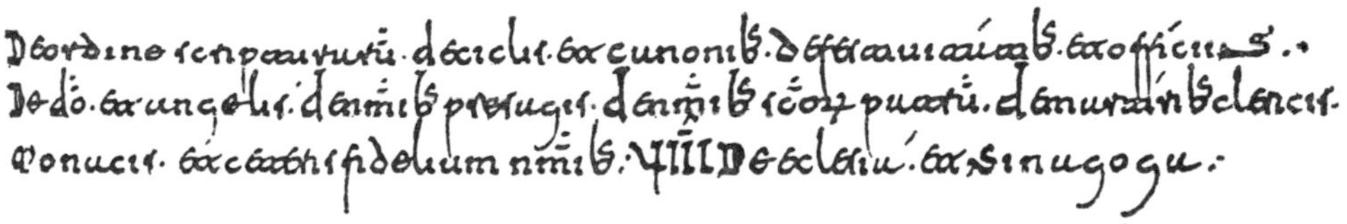

Visigothic script, 9th or 10th century.

Beneventan script, c. 1087.

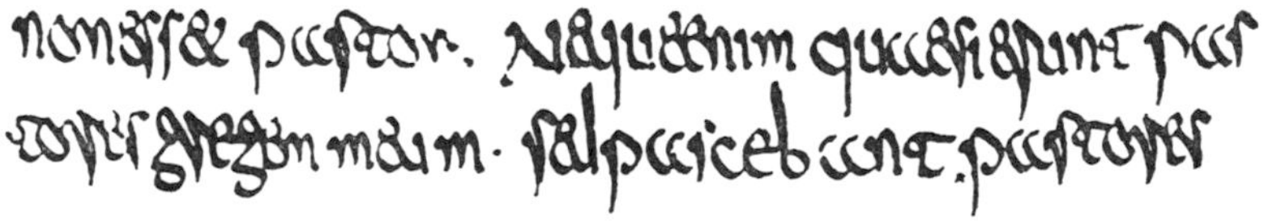

Merovingian script, Luxeuil type, 7th–8th century.

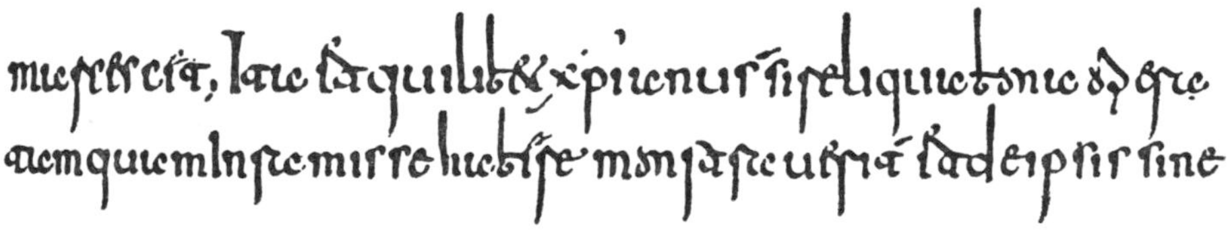

Merovingian script, "ab-type" Corbie, 8th century.

17

Et ecce uir nomine ioseph· qui erat decurio
uir bonus et iustus hic non consenserat con
silium et acceribus eorum· ab con machia

supra dic tas: nov em bres: sic tem
pere ā hortes· ut:uigiliccrum agen
dec:par uissimo inter uallo quo

by side, a majuscule and a minuscule ("lower case") type, each being a different combination of the same ancient elements. Majuscule would appear to be of slightly earlier date; later scribes treated this script as more dignified. It is perhaps not a mere coincidence (although this possibility cannot be excluded) that the earliest surviving manuscript in Irish majuscule, the *Cathach* of St. Columba (now deposited in the Royal Irish Academy, Dublin) dates, in all probability, from the end of the sixth century, whereas the earliest extant minuscule, the Antiphonary of Bangor (now at Milan, Ambrosian Library, C.5 inf.) dates from a century later (680–691). A third type, which is best described as "cursive minuscule", differs from formal minuscule only in degree; it was often used for textbooks and for Gospel books of small size—the sort of book a travelling scholar or missionary might conveniently carry in his satchel *(cumdach)*. Of this kind are such "pocket Gospel books" as the Book of Dimma and the Book of Moling (both at Trinity College, Dublin), or Codex Bonifatianus 3 at Fulda. The lettering is very small and compact, ligatures and abbreviations are employed most liberally, and every possible device is used in order to save space; in this way the scribe manages to accommodate even a text of considerable length on a comparatively small number of pages.

Small initials from the *Cathach* of St. Columba.

ILLUMINATION   The earliest surviving manuscript of Irish origin, the *Cathach*, has very little ornament; however, its simple hollow initials, ending in small spirals and often surrounded by lines of dots, show already some of the rudiments of later illuminative art. In the second half of the seventh century the utilitarian type of codex, sparsely ornamented, of which the Gospels known as Usserianus Primus (Trinity College, Dublin) or the Antiphonary of Bangor are good examples, begins to be overshadowed by

Initial of XPI AUTEM GENERATIO in the Book of Durrow.

such works of art as the Book of Durrow (Trinity College, Dublin, MS 57). This Gospel manuscript is named after the monastery of Durrow in Central Ireland, a foundation of St. Columba, where it was kept from the eleventh century, if not earlier. In this codex the artistic type of the Irish Gospel book is seen already fully developed: each Gospel is preceded by the symbol of the respective evangelist in an ornamental frame, by a page of rich ornament, and (as opening of the text) by an initial in a matching style. At the beginning of the book are found a page with a complicated cross ornament, another page with the symbols of the four evangelists in the corners of a cross, and tables of the Eusebian Canons in ornamental frames; at the end there is an ornamental page with a pattern of squares. Apart from the opening passages of the four Gospels, there are ornamental initials in two other places; they bring into relief the XPI AUTEM GENERATIO (after the genealogy of Jesus in Matthew) and the FUIT IN DIEBUS HERODIS after the prologue of Luke. Ornamented initials on a smaller scale occur here and there in the prefatory matter. The ornamentation of the codex is planned in every detail; a very similar plan, though more developed, underlies the ornamentation of the much admired Book of Kells (Trinity College, Dublin, MS 58) and the Lindisfarne Gospels (British Museum, MS Cotton Nero D. IV). This plan of illumination set the fashion for many a fine Gospel book in Northumbria and on the Continent. A well-designed plan such as this must have originated either in the mind of an individual or within a closely knit spitirual community. In any event, it must be the product of a very definite spiritual and artistic milieu. One cannot help thinking in this connexion of that great community of Irish monks, the *familia Columcille*. The manuscript might have actually been written at Durrow, but on this question the opinions of the experts are divided. It appears to have been one of the earliest masterpieces of its kind, and might well have been the very first.

The "vocabulary" of ornamental motifs draws on sources of widely different origin. There are the inherited spirals and "trumpets" of Celtic art, which, like the millefiori and cloisonné work, were transferred from metal and enamel to the book page. As early as the *Cathach* we find also the use of dot edging. In *Durrow*, these rows of dots are seen not only around the contours of letters but also superimposed on interlacing ribbon; scattered or in small groups (preferably in groups of three), they also serve the purpose of filling empty space. The earliest instance of this type of ornamentation that we know is in the Vienna codex of the *Materia Medica* of Dioscurides, a *manuscrit de luxe* written at Constantinople in 512, of apparently Greco-Oriental origin. The most striking ornamental feature in *Durrow* is, however, the broad band interlacing, framed by double lines, which has its counterpart

Celtic "trumpet" pattern

in stone on the (slightly later) cross of Fahan Mura and, later still, on the silver shrine of the Domnach Airgid manuscript in the Royal Irish Academy. This broad band interlacing soon gave way to a narrow thread or string interlacing. Interlacing of one kind or another is found in medieval art over a wide area; however, it seems to be significant that band interlacing as a frame of the written page occurs first in the Syriac Gospels of Rabula (now in the Laurentian Library, Florence), and later in Coptic manuscripts of the eighth and ninth centuries. Another link with Coptic and Syriac art in the illumination of the Book of Durrow is the predominant colour scheme of red, green, and yellow; the artist of Durrow sets these colours off by the use of a deep black for the background and for the filling of blanks. Special mention must be made of folio 192 verso, which faces the opening page of St. John. On this page, a circular medallion, which forms the centre of the composition, is surrounded by friezes of animal interlacing. The centre-piece, which has a close Coptic parallel and a long iconographic pedigree, has been plausibly explained by Victor H. Elbern as a Trinitarian symbol. The animal interlacing, on the other hand, is the first appearance in Irish illumination of a characteristic motif of Teutonic art. The most likely place for artistic contacts between Celts and Teutons would seem to have been Northumbria. But even here, at its first occurrence in an Irish manuscript, the motif is treated with a difference. Not only is the individual animal more isolated, not to say independent, and less twisted than is common in Germanic art; it also retains more of its anatomy, as is exemplified by the comparatively naturalistic treatment of the legs. The difference becomes evident to anyone who compares the *Durrow* page with the animal interlacing on metal from the Sutton Hoo find in the British Museum. This greater vitality in ornamental animals is characteristic of Irish art for a long time, both in metal and on the vellum page: its animal bodies, however drawn-out, sinuous, and contorted they may be, at least always have heads and extremities that give some impression of realism. Among the smaller drawings in the Book of Kells, where the principle of abstraction was not so strictly adhered to, we find, in the work of one particular illuminator, most appealing representations of animals—hound and hare, fish and otter, and many others—in quite a realistic style.

Shoulder-buckle with animal interlacing and geometrical ornament in millefiori-work from the ship burial of Sutton Hoo, British Museum, and animal interlacing on a clasp, from the same find.
Opposite: Folio 192 V of the Book of Durrow.

Initial and display script in the Book of Durrow:
INITIUM EVANGELII IHU XPI.

A link between script and illumination is established by ornamental initials. Unlike the early continental scribes, who, regardless of the context, put an enlarged capital at the beginning of a page or even of a column, the Irish scribe and illuminator, however keen he may be on decorating his manuscript, does not for a moment forget that the initial is part of the text and that it should be used as a means to its articulation. This idea already dominates the ornamentation of the *Cathach:* each psalm begins with an initial; the letters immediately following are not written in the ordinary text hand, but form a transition, in both size and elaboration, from the one to the other. The same is done in the Book of Durrow and in the other illuminated manuscripts of the Irish and Anglo-Saxon schools, only in a more elaborate and sophisticated form. In *Durrow*, for example, the large initial, which grows in size and richness of ornament from one Gospel to the next, is regularly followed by a smaller initial of the same style, which in turn is continued by one or more lines of ornamental script framed by a band or dotted oblong. In *Durrow* these letters are normally hollow, with filling in colour or in black, and they are always, by various devices, united into one artistic unit. For this ornamental script, which has a parallel in the Cufic script of Islamic art, a special alphabet was often employed, which is found also in inscriptions; most letter-forms are angular, and all curves are broken at sharp angles. This alphabet survived until the Franco-insular book illumination of the Carolingian period. Large initials are integrated into this "display script" and sometimes (for example, if some part of the letter, such as the tail of a Q, extends far towards the bottom of the page), are connected even with the ordinary text hand, by lines of dots or rows of interlinking pot-hooks in red ink. The text itself is divided into units of subject-matter by small sized initials, usually in black, surrounded by a border of red dots. In manuscripts of the highest class, for example in the Book of Kells, even these small initials are relatively more elaborate; those of *Kells* in particular give evidence of the scribe's almost inexhaustible inventiveness. In similar manner, though less extravagantly, some scribes (especially in the Book of Kells) decorated ends of paragraphs.

Ornamental
line-end from
the Book of Kells.

22

FUIT HOMO MISSUS A DEO

cui nomen erat Iohannis hic uenit

The freedom with which part of a letter is allowed to blossom out into some ornamental feature (spiral, cross), into a plant or even an animal (the "tongue" of *E* or *F*, for example, has often the shape of a fish) is characteristic of the art of early Ireland. The Irish artist does not strive for the "closed form" of classical Mediterranean art. Design and background are interchangeable, a ribbon can form a cross, an ornamental composition and its frame may merge into one another, details suddenly become independent of the whole, and the human body, especially hair and beard, and the clothes by which it is covered, tend to be treated geometrically.

Initial line in ornamental script: FUIT HOMO..., in MS A.II.17, fol. 2 V, of Durham Cathedral.

In this lack of constraint, in the ambiguity and protean gift of metamorphosis of the several elements of a larger composition, and generally in the trend towards the ornamental and the abstract, Irish art reveals a structure of mind which it would be difficult, if not impossible, to describe accurately. Analogous phenomena, however, are recognizable in other fields of early Irish culture. The formality of protocol at the courts of Old Irish saga, which leaves Homeric etiquette far behind; the minute distinctions of personal status in Irish legal texts; the complicated internal rhyme, which overlaps the verse structure, in early Irish lyrics; the sublime remoteness (which later, however, degenerates into stereotyped artificiality) of Irish bardic poetry, far beyond anything even in Pindar; the endeavour of Irish commentators and textbook writers on every discipline to give more than one explanation for one and the same thing: all these phenomena are more or less parallel. What influence may this mental structure have had on the way in which the Irish assimilated Christianity? The question cannot be answered in this general form. Even when it comes to particular cultural phenomena, the answer will seldom be more than tentative. It is certainly to be expected that analogous tendencies may be observed in the selection of elements of ancient culture which appealed to the Irish mind (for example, the love of classification, which is apparent in Boethius) as well as in their own contributions (for example, the "cyclic" concept of time in the Irish liturgy as against the linear historical concept of time in the Roman liturgy). At the moment we have to be content with such intimations. Some of the suggestions which I have made will be elaborated in the chapters that follow.

Ornament in the Book of Kells.

The chief monasteries of early medieval Ireland.

THE IRISH MONASTERIES

ONKS and "virgins of Christ" were a prominent feature of the Irish Church from the earliest times. In his *Confession* St. Patrick refers to them as proof of his successful apostolate. Little, however, is known about the details of Irish monastic life in those days. The monks probably lived as hermits, either singly or in small colonies. Women who had made a vow of chastity often ministered to the needs of the clergy in Patrick's churches. From the *Catalogus Sanctorum Hiberniae* we learn that the saints of the "First Order", that is to say, Patrick and his contemporaries, neither refused the service of women nor objected to their company. "Building firmly on the rock which is Christ, they did not fear the storms of temptation." Kuno Meyer, and even Dom Louis Gougaud, interpreted this statement as a reference to "spiritual marriage". This ancient Christian custom, which was condemned by the Church as early as the Council of Nicaea, allowed a cleric or hermit to live together with a "syneis-akte" *(virgo subintroducta)*. In the opinion of Meyer and Gougaud, this custom survived in Ireland for centuries after its official ecclesiastical condemnation. Such an interpretation, however, is not warranted either by the *Catalogus Sanctorum* or by the accounts of Patrick's ecclesiastical foundations as recorded by Tírechán in the seventh century. The tenth-century poem to Crínóg, in which an ageing hermit ostensibly welcomes the return of a lady with whom he has slept as a boy of seven, is, according to James Carney, an allegory—Crínóg, the lady of the poem, is in reality a psalter!

In the early Irish Church religious persons of different sex were severely restricted in their personal relations. The ninth canon of the *Synod of St. Patrick* decrees as follows:

"A monk and a virgin, he from one place and she from another, shall not spend the night in the same inn or drive from one place to another in the same carriage or engage in long conversations."

In the legend of St. Patrick we read the following story: One of Patrick's disciples, Bishop Mél, lived together with a kinswoman. People began to gossip about them, and Patrick found it necessary to intervene. He soon became convinced of Mél's and the woman's innocence, but nevertheless advised them to separate "lest the weak be scandalized and the name of God be blasphemed through our fault". In St. Brigit's church at Kildare the men and women of the congregation were separated by a wall of timber which ran along the centre of the nave.

Patrick, as we have seen, repeatedly speaks of monks, but he never mentions monasteries. The last canon of the *Synod of St. Patrick*, which forbids a monk to move elsewhere without his abbot's permission, was apparently added at a later time. One of Patrick's disciples, the skilled bronze-smith Assicus, is, however, represented by Tírechán as the head of a monastic community. At one time he secretly retired to a solitary place, but his monks, like the disciples of St. Anthony the Hermit, discovered his retreat and forced him to rejoin them. That as early as the first generation after Patrick Irish monasticism began to be more strictly organized is suggested *inter alia* by the fact that Bishop Cormac of Armagh (d. 497) is termed "abbot" in the Book of Leinster. If this terminology goes back to Cormac's time it might be explained on the assumption that Cormac reorganized the Chapter of Armagh as a quasi-monastic community. A contemporary of Cormac, St. Enda, is said to have been given land for the foundation of a monastery on Ára-mór, the largest of the Aran Islands, by Oengus mac Nadfráich, king of Munster (d. 490 or 491). About the same time St. Brigit, who according to the Annals died in 524 or 528, must have founded the double monastery (one part for men, the other for women) at Kildare, which was to become one of the most famous monastic centres of Ireland.

The great wave of monastic foundations in Ireland falls, however, in the sixth century. It started from Wales.

Tradition has it that some of the early founders of monasteries in Ireland, namely Finnian of Clonard, Ciarán of Clonmacnoise, Brendan of Clonfert, and Columba (Columcille), were disciples of St. Enda. The Life of this saint was, however, written centuries after his time and its historical value is rather doubtful. In religion as in other walks of life, the posthumous fame of an impressive personality is often enhanced by representing other famous men as his disciples. Enda, who was the first to retire not only into solitude but to one of those forbidding rocky islands off the west coast, must have deeply impressed his contemporaries and gained a reputation for sanctity even in his lifetime. Finnian too appears in later legend as the master of many other saints, in particular of the "twelve apostles of Ireland"—a group of sixth-century saints whose names vary to some extent in tradition.

Prominent among Welsh saints who had connexions with Ireland was Gildas, author of a work *On the Fall of Britain* and of a short monastic Penitential. He is supposed to have visited Ireland in 565; even before that visit a certain Vennia(n)us, possibly Finnian of Clonard, had consulted him on a point of ecclesiastical discipline and had received an answer in writing. St. Brendan, as we are told in his *Vita*, travelled to Britain in order to visit Gildas. The Penitential of Gildas has come down to us in an Irish redaction; according to some historians it is actually the work of an Irishman. The same is true of the *Extracts from a Book of David*, which also is penitential in character. The saint in question is, of course, St. Dewi of Menevia.

The foundation dates of many Irish monasteries are known, either accurately or approximately, from the Annals. The foundation of Clonard by St. Finnian (d. 549) must date from before 515 because of the saint's connexion with the churches of Leinster; after that date the Upper Boyne district, where Clonard is situated, had fallen to the Northern Uí Néill. Clonmacnoise on the Shannon, one of the most wealthy monasteries in Ireland, and a centre of national as well as Latin learning, was founded by Ciarán, "the carpenter's son", between 540 and 550. About the middle of the sixth century or soon afterwards (555 or 559) Comgall founded Bangor on the southern shore of Belfast Loch, and Brendan founded Clonfert in Connacht (558 or 564). Columba, who belonged to the royal family of the Uí Néill, founded several monasteries in Ireland, including Durrow and Derry, and afterwards (563 or 565) emigrated to the west coast of Scotland, where he founded the island monastery of Iona (Hy). A younger generation of monks is represented by Coemgen (Kevin), the founder of Glendalough in Co. Wicklow, Maedóc, the founder of Ferns in South Leinster, and Carthach, the founder of Lismore in Munster; they all died in the first third of the seventh century.

Side by side with the older foundations, such as Armagh, Kildare, or Aran, these monasteries soon became the ecclesiastical and intellectual centres of Ireland. Some of these, Bangor for example, occasionally sent a number of their monks away to found new monasteries elsewhere. A mother-house and its daughter-houses, as well as all monasteries and churches that had the same founder, formed monastic "families". Such monastic *paruchiae*, some being of considerable extent, power, and influence, were known from the seventh century onwards: for instance the *paruchiae* of Kildare and Clonmacnoise, and above all the *familia Columcille*, which comprised the numerous monasteries founded by that saint. During the later seventh century Armagh made an attempt at uniting in like manner all the churches founded, or supposed to have been founded, by St. Patrick.

We know in considerable detail the lay-out and organization of the early Irish monasteries and the life which their inmates had to lead. Our sources are partly ruins and excavations, partly the works of hagiographical and ascetical writers. Unfortunately most of the literary sources are late, and what they tell us of the monastic life in their own day must not be uncritically presumed to apply to earlier periods, let alone the times of the founders.

Monastic settlements were normally surrounded by strong circular walls. They consisted of a number of separate buildings: church, refectory, school, guest-house, and cells which as a rule would house two or three monks each. The most common building materials were timber or wattles, and reeds for roofing. These perishable materials are largely responsible for the fact that so little of ancient monastic buildings, and of the literary and artistic treasures which they once housed, has been preserved. In the west and south of the country only, on the bare and stony islands off the Irish coast, did the monks have to build in stone. They did so in a primitive manner, without the use of mortar, but their building technique was a match for the rough climate. Best preserved of all is the monastic site on Skellig Rock (St. Michael's, Sceilg Mhichíl) in the Atlantic Ocean, about twenty-two miles south-west of Ireland. There, on the edge of a 700-foot precipice, sheltered from the northern storms and facing the south, were found six cells and two churches within a ring wall, apparently of early date, as well as the ruins of a church of later times. We know that the monastery existed at the beginning of the ninth century, but it may be considerably older. A study of the building technique of St. Michael's is very instructive. Evidently the technique of building in wood and other light materials has been adapted, in an archaic manner, to the art of building in stone. The cells, here as elsewhere in ancient Ireland, have the shape of beehives. The dome consists of layers of hewn stone in progressively

Beehive Cell on
St. Michael's Rock.

narrowing circles, topped by a single stone. The churches, like most early Irish churches, are very small. (To this day, in the more remote parts of Ireland, the men attend Mass outside the church-door —a polite gesture to the ladies, which dates from times when church buildings were normally too small to hold the entire congregation.) Even when a monastic community grew to large numbers, which was often the case, the size of the church did not increase proportionately; there was a preference for building several small ones. There still exist in Ireland several hundred small stone churches, dating from the eighth to the tenth century. They are modelled on earlier churches which were made of timber planks. Their roofs are steep; the gables are formed of rows of beautifully carved stones. This type of church served as a model for reliquaries. The artist who painted the Temptation of Christ in the Book of Kells has given this familiar shape even to the Temple of Jerusalem, which is the scene of the last temptation.

Nevertheless large stone churches were not entirely unknown in Ireland during the eighth and ninth centuries. Cases in point are Our Lady's Church and the so-called Cathedral in Glendalough, and the church in Banagher, Co. Derry (which has, however, undergone extensive reconstruction). A seventh-century church of large dimensions, though not preserved, is known from the description of an eye-witness, Cogitosus, author of a life of St. Brigit, who describes the great church at Kildare in the following terms:

There (at Kildare) repose the glorious bodies of both Archbishop Conled and the noble virgin Brigit in their sarcophagi, the one to the right and the other to the left of a beautifully adorned altar. These sarcophagi are richly decorated with gold, silver, and multicoloured precious stones; they have also pictorial representations in relief and in colours, and are surmounted by crowns of gold and silver. The church, however, is not the original one: a new church has been erected in the place of the old one, in order to hold the increased number of the faithful. Its ground-plan is large, and it rises to a dizzy height. It is adorned with painted tablets. The interior contains three large oratories, divided from one another by walls of timber, but all under one roof. One wall, covered with linen curtains and decorated with paintings, traverses the eastern part of the church from one side to the other. There are doors in it at either end. The one door gives access to the sanctuary and the altar, where the bishop, with his school of clerics (regularis schola) and those who are called to the celebration of the holy mysteries, offers the divine sacrifice to the Lord. By the other door of the dividing wall, the abbess enters with her virgins and with pious widows in order to participate in the Supper of Jesus Christ, which is His flesh and blood. The remainder of the building is divided lengthwise into two equal parts by another wall, which runs from the western side to the transverse wall. The church has many windows.

Priests and lay persons of the male sex enter by an ornamented door on the right-hand side; matrons and virgins enter by another door on the left-hand side. In this way the one basilica is sufficient for a huge crowd, separated by walls according to state, grade and sex, but united in the Spirit, to pray to the almighty Lord.

This description is interesting in two respects. Firstly, we learn that the church of the double monastery was also the place of worship for the people of the surrounding district. It must have been for the purpose of accommodating these crowds that the structural alterations—virtually amounting to a new church, as Cogitosus tells us in another chapter—were undertaken. The original church had probably been built only for the nuns and monks of Brigit's double monastery, and had separate entrances only for these two groups of worshippers. The new church was so designed that not only the monks and nuns of the monastic establishment but also the secular clergy and the laity, men and women, were kept strictly apart. Another detail of considerable interest is the separation, by a transverse wall, of the "choir" and the "people". Cogitosus' description is reminiscent of the "iconostasis" of eastern churches. Similar was the plan of a church (described by Bede, *Vita Abbatum*, c. 6) which Benedict Biscop began to build at Wearmouth in Northumbria in 674. There also the width of the church was divided by a wooden wall covered with sacred pictures.

TOMBSTONES A monk was normally buried within the precincts of the monastery where he had lived. Some of the large and celebrated monasteries had burial places also for their patrons and benefactors. Their names were entered in the diptychs of the altar and were regularly recited, along with the names of the founder and his successors, at the *Memento mortuorum* of the Mass. Tombstones, occasionally in the archaic Ogam script (an alphabet consisting of groups of straight lines which were cut into a slab along its edge), but normally in Irish majuscule, have been preserved on many monastic sites. They are most numerous at Clonmacnoise. Apart from the common Christian symbols, the cross and the chrismon (monogram of Christ), both frequently inscribed in a circle, we encounter on these slabs all the ornamental motives of Irish Christian art. The text usually consists of a brief conventional

Skellig Rock (St. Michael's), Co. Kerry, with ruins of the ancient monastery.

Old church ("House of St. Columcille") at Kells.

Reliquary from Lough Erne.

formula of the type *Or(oit) do Aigidiu-'* (Say) a prayer for Aigide' (from a slab at Durrow). Just as in classical antiquity, the dead person addresses, as it were, the passer-by. The ornamentation of the Durrow stone consists of a ringed cross, partly filled with interlacing. This is the typical "Irish cross", which from the eighth century to the present day has dominated the graveyards of Ireland.

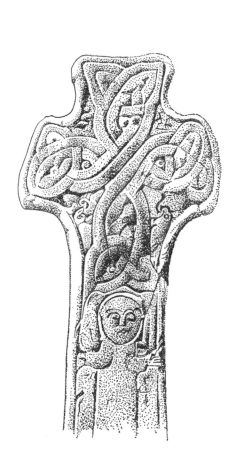

The Old Irish stone crosses of Carndonagh and Fahan Mura, in Donegal, 7th century.

HIGH CROSSES

The ancient monastic "high crosses" have an entirely different significance: they mark places of special devotion. The Gospel manuscript known as the Book of Moling contains at the end some liturgical texts and a plan of the monastery of Tech-Moling, where it was apparently written. This monastic "map" shows the circular wall around the monastery, and, among other details, twelve crosses, some within the wall and some outside. These crosses were dedicated to the prophets and the evangelists, to Christ and His apostles, to the Holy Spirit and to the Angels. In the early period such crosses were characteristic of Ireland's central plain. The most important ones are found at Ahenny (Co. Tipperary), Slievenaman (Kilkenny), and Clonmacnoise on the Shannon; there are none in Northern Ireland, but there are some in Scotland (Iona) and in the Isle of Man. It is not until the late ninth and tenth centuries, the period of the big and richly decorated high crosses, that the North of Ireland is well represented.

The monks had to submit to strict rules, in which the spirit of early Eastern monasticism survived unbroken. Unfortunately no early monastic rule of the Irish homeland has been preserved in its original form. The *Rule of St. Ailbe* (the founder of Imlech, now Emly, in the south of Ireland) is an Old Irish poem in quatrains which appears to have been compiled out of several independent texts. On philological grounds, it has been assigned a date between 700 and 950. With its insistence on silence, strict abstinence, long hours of prayer, and particularly on an elaborate ritual of prostrations at the canonical hours and on many other occasions it testifies to very old monastic practices. More directly authentic, however, is a work which we still read substantially in the form in which it was written towards the end of the sixth century—the *Rule of Saint Columbanus*. This first pioneer of Irish Christianity on the Continent wrote his rule for the monasteries which he had founded in France and Italy, mainly Luxeuil and Bobbio. It stands to reason, however, that Columbanus, as far as was feasible, would have modelled his rule on that of the monastery of Bangor from which he had come, and this surmise is confirmed by the similarity of the sacred office as laid down in Columbanus' Rule and that which underlies the Antiphonary of Bangor. Echoes of the rules of St. Basil and of Cassian bring into relief the contacts between Irish and Eastern monasticism. The *Rule of St. Columbanus* is composed of two separate texts which together form a larger unit: a "Rule for Monks" and a "Communal Rule". The former treats of the spiritual life of the monk in its more specific sense: of obedience, silence, abstinence from food and drink, poverty, chastity, and mortification; this series of spiritual counsels is once interrupted by a long chapter on the chanting of psalms, especially during the protracted Saturday and Sunday vigils, which are the next best thing to a *laus perennis*. The "Communal Rule" (which does not seem to have been known at Bobbio) goes into more detail; it fixes severe punishments and penances for even the minutest breaches of monastic discipline. In spite of a later revision (of which the first nine chapters are on the whole free) this Communal Rule with all its details unfolds to us a most interesting picture of day-to-day life in the Irish monastery.

HE MONKS' RULE OF ST. COLUMBAN THE ABBOT

First of all things we are taught to love God with the whole heart and the whole mind and all our strength, and our neighbour as ourselves; next come our works.

1. Of Obedience

At the first word of a senior, all on hearing should rise to obey, since their obedience is shown to God, as our Lord Jesus Christ says: He who hears you hears Me. Therefore if anyone hearing the word does not rise at once, he is to be judged disobedient. But he who answers back incurs the charge of insubordination, and thus is not only guilty of disobedience, but also, by opening the way of answering back for others, is to be regarded as the destroyer of many. Yet if any murmurs, he too, as though not obeying heartily, must be considered disobedient. Therefore let his work be rejected, until his good will be made known. But up to what measure is obedience laid down? Up to death it is assuredly enjoined, since Christ obeyed the Father up to death for us.... Thus nothing must be refused in their obedience by Christ's true disciples, however hard and difficult it be, but it must be seized with zeal, and even with gladness, since if obedience is not of this nature, it will not be pleasing to the Lord....

2. Of Silence

The rule of silence is decreed to be carefully observed, since it is written: *But the nurture of righteousness is silence and peace.* And thus, lest one be apprehended as guilty of much talking, it is needful that one keep silence, except for things profitable and necessary, since according to Scripture, *in many words sin will not be lacking* (Proverbs 10.19). Therefore the Saviour says: *By thy words thou shalt be justified, and by thy words thou shalt be condemned* (Matthew 12.37). Justly will they be damned who would not say just things when they could, but preferred to say with garrulous loquacity what is evil, unjust, irreverent, empty, harmful, dubious, false, provocative, disparaging, base, fanciful, blasphemous, rude, and tortuous. Therefore we must keep silence on these and kindred matters, and speak with care and prudence, lest either disparagements or swollen oppositions should break out in vicious garrulity.

3. Of Food and Drink

Let the monks' food be poor and taken in the evening, such as to avoid repletion, and their drink such as to avoid intoxication, so that it may both maintain life and not harm (their souls): vegetables, beans, flour mixed with water, together with the small bread of a loaf, lest the stomach be burdened and the mind confused. For indeed those who desire eternal rewards must only consider usefulness and use. Use of life must be moderated just as toil must be moderated, since this is true discretion, that the possibility of spiritual progress may be kept with a temperance that punishes the flesh. For if abstinence exceeds measure, it will be a vice and not a virtue; for virtue maintains and contains many goods. Therefore we must fast daily, just as we must feed daily....

6. Of Chastity

A monk's chastity is judged in his thoughts, and to him, along with the disciples who approached to hear, it is doubtless said by the Lord: *He who looks on a woman to lust after her has already defiled her in his heart* (Matthew 5.28). For while his vow is weighed by Him to whom he is devoted, there is cause to fear lest He should find in the soul something to loathe; lest perhaps according to the opinion of St. Peter (2 Peter 2.14) they have *eyes full of wantonness and of adultery.* And what profit is it if he be virgin in body, if he be not virgin in mind? For God, being Spirit, dwells in the spirit and the mind which He has seen undefiled, in which there is no adulterous thought, no stain of a spirit polluted, and no spot of sin.

7. Of the Choir Office

Concerning the synaxis, that is, the office of psalms and prayers in canonical manner, detailed directions must be given, since its observance has been variously bequeathed to us by different authorities. Thus, in accordance with the nature of man's life and the succession of the seasons, I also shall draw up in writing a (seasonally) varying observance. For, in view of the mutual changes of the seasons, it should not be stereotyped; it is fitting that it be longer on the long nights and shorter on the short ones. Hence, in agreement with our predecessors, (we prescribe that) from the twenty-fourth day of June onwards, while the nights increase, the office is to begin to grow gradually from twelve chants, the shortest measure on the nights of the Sabbath or the Lord's Day, up to the beginning of winter, that is, the first of November. By that time they sing twenty-five psalms with antiphons, which always follow in the third place after two chanted psalms, in such a way that within the aforesaid nights they sing the entire psalter, while on the remaining nights of the whole winter they are content with twelve chants. From winter's end, gradually throughout the spring, three psalms are always dropped so that only twelve antiphons remain on the holy nights (of Saturday and Sunday), that is, the thirty-six psalms of the daily winter office, but twenty-four (on all other nights) throughout the whole spring and summer and up to the autumn equinox, that is, the twenty-fourth of September. Then the synaxis is again like that on the spring equinox, that is, the twenty-fifth of March. Thus by mutual changes it slowly grows and lessens.

Thus we must weigh our watching according to our strength, especially when we are bidden by the Author of our salvation to watch and pray at all times, and when Paul ordains: Pray without ceasing (1 Thess. 5.17). But since we must know the measure of canonical prayers, in which all gather together at appointed hours in common prayer, at the conclusion of which each should pray in his own cell, our predecessors have appointed three psalms at each of the day-time hours, considering the work to be done in between, together with an addition of versicles which intercede first for our own sins, then for all Christian people, then for priests and the other orders of the holy flock that are consecrate to God, finally for those that give alms, next for the concord of kings, lastly for our enemies, that God reckon it not to them for sin that they persecute and slander us, since they know not what they do. But at night-fall twelve psalms are chanted, and at midnight twelve likewise; but towards morning twice ten and twice two are appointed, as has been said, during the season of short nights, while more, as I have already said, are always ordained for the night of the Lord's Day and Sabbath vigil, on which seventy-five are sung individually in the course of one office....

9. Of Mortification
The chief part of the monks' rule is mortification, since indeed they are enjoined in Scripture, Do nothing without counsel. Thus if nothing is to be done without counsel, everything must be asked for by counsel. Thus we are enjoined through Moses also (Deuteronomy 32.7), Ask thy father and he will show thee, thy elders and they will tell thee. But though this training seem hard to the hard-hearted, namely that a man should always hang upon the lips of another, yet by those who are fixed in their fear of God it will be found pleasant and safe, if it is kept wholly and not in part, since nothing is pleasanter than safety of conscience and nothing safer than exoneration of the soul, which none can provide for himself by his own efforts, since it properly belongs to the judgement of others. For what the judge's examination has already tried is free from the fear of censure, and on him is laid the weight of another's burden, and he bears the peril of all that he undertakes; for, as it is written, the peril of the judge is greater than that of the accused. So anyone who has always asked, if he follows will never err, since if the other's reply has erred, there will be no error in the faith of him who believes and the toil of him who obeys, nor will they lack the reward of his asking. If, on the other hand, he has considered anything by himself when he ought to have asked, he is proved guilty of error in this very fact, that he dared to judge when he ought to have been judged; even though it turn out right, it will be reckoned to him as wrong, since he has departed from the right course in this; for the man to whose duty it belongs only to obey presumes to judge nothing by himself....

There is a threefold way of mortification: not to disagree in mind, not to speak as one pleases with the tongue, not to go anywhere with complete freedom. This means, always to say to a senior, however adverse his instructions, Not as I will but as thou wilt (Matthew 26.39), following the example of the Lord and Saviour, Who says, I came down from heaven, not to do My will, but the will of Him who sent Me, the Father.... (John 6.38).

Opposite: Two Irish high crosses of the 9th and 10th centuries: east view of "Flan's Cross" and west view of the "Cross of the Scriptures", both at Clonmacnoise, Co. Offaly.

It has been ordained, my dearest brethren, by the holy fathers that we make confession before mealtime or before entering our beds or whenever it is opportune, since confession and penance free from death. Therefore not even the very small sins are to be omitted from confession, since, as it is written (Sirach 19.1), He who omits small things gradually declines.

Thus him who has not waited for grace at table and has not responded Amen, it is ordained to correct with six blows. Likewise him who has spoken while eating, unless because of the wants of another brother, it is ordained to correct with six blows. And him who has not blessed the spoon with which he sups, and him who has spoken with a shout, that is, has talked in a louder tone than the usual, with six blows.

If he has not blessed the lamp, that is, when it is lighted by a younger brother and is not presented to a senior for his blessing, with six blows. If he has called anything his own, with six blows. Let him who has cut the table with a knife be corrected with ten blows.

Whoever of the brethren, to whom the care of cooking or serving has been entrusted, has spilt any drop, it is ordained to correct him by prayer in church after the end of the office, so that the brethren pray for him. Let him who has forgotten the prostration at the synaxis, that is, at the office, namely the prostration in church after the end of each psalm, do penance likewise. In the same manner let him who has lost the crumbs be corrected by prayer in church; yet this small penance is only to be assigned to him, if it is something small that he has spilt.

But if through negligence or forgetfulness or failure of care he has lost more than usual either of fluids or of solids, let him do penance with a long pardon in church by prostrating himself without moving any limb while they sing twelve psalms at the twelfth hour.

Or certainly if it is much that he spilt, according to the measures of beer or portions of whatever things he has lost in spilling through the occurrence of neglect, let him supply for an equal number of days what he had been accustomed to receive lawfully for his own use, and know that he has lost them to his cost, for example, that he drink water in place of beer. For what is spilt on the table and runs off it, we say that it suffices to seek pardon from one's seat.

Him who on leaving the house has not prostrated himself to ask a prayer, and after receiving a blessing has not blessed himself, (and) him who has not approached the cross, it is ordained to correct with twelve blows. Likewise him who has forgotten the prayer before work or after work, with twelve blows. And him who has eaten without a blessing, with twelve blows. And let him who on returning home has not bowed himself within the house to ask a prayer, be corrected with twelve blows. But the brother who has confessed all these things and others as far as deserves a special fast, with half penance....

Him who through a cough has not chanted well at the beginning of a psalm, it is ordained to correct with six blows. Likewise him who has bitten the cup of salvation with his teeth, with six blows. Him who has not followed the order for the sacrifice, with six blows. And him who is smiling at the synaxis, that is, at the office of prayers, with six blows; if his laughter has broken out aloud, with a special fast, unless it has happened pardonably. He who with unclean hands receives the blessed bread, with twelve blows. He who forgets to make the oblation right until they go to Mass, with a hundred blows.

He who tells idle tales to another, if he censures himself at once, with a mere pardon; but if he has not censured himself, with an imposition of silence or fifty blows. He who brings forward a simple excuse, when examination is made of something, and does not at once say in begging pardon, It is my fault, I am sorry, with fifty blows. He who sets counsel against counsel, with fifty blows. He who has struck the altar, with fifty blows....

He who has replied to a brother on his pointing something out, It is not as you say, except for seniors speaking honestly to juniors, with an imposition of silence or fifty blows; this only to be allowed, that he should reply to his brother of equal standing, if there is something nearer the truth than what the other says and he remembers

Opposite: Cliffs of the Aran Islands: Inishmore, with the ruins of the "Black Fortress".

it, If you recollect rightly, my brother, and the other on hearing this does not repeat his assertion, but humbly says, *I trust that you remember better; I have erred in speech by forgetfulness, and am sorry that I said ill.* These are the words of the sons of God, if nothing be in rivalry, as the apostle says (Philipp. 2.3), nor in vain glory, but in lowliness of spirit each reckoning the other better than himself. But let him who has excused himself be considered, not a spiritual son of God, but a carnal son of Adam....

He who utters a loud speech to censure the porter's work, (saying) that the porter has not kept the hours well, with an imposition of silence or fifty blows. And he who conceals some fault when he sees it in his brother, until he is reproved over another failing or over the same, and then brings it forward against his brother, with three special fasts. Let him who corrects or slanders other brothers' works, do penance with three special fasts. Let him who utters reproof against reproof, that is, who chides one who is chiding him, likewise do penance with three special fasts.

He who slanders a brother, or hears one slandering, and does not correct him, with three special fasts. He who utters some abuse with spleen, let him likewise do penance with three special fasts. He who in censuring something does not wish to make it known to his immediate superior, (but waits) until he may disclose it to the senior father, with three special fasts, unless all these things arise out of a confession made in modesty. If a brother has been melancholy, if he can contain himself, let him keep back his confession for the meanwhile, so that he may speak more devoutly, when the melancholy has ceased....

He who advises a relative among the brethren, who is learning some skill or anything enjoined by the seniors, that he should rather learn reading, three special fasts.

He who dares to say to his immediate superior, *You shall not judge my case, but our senior,* or the remaining brethren, or, *We will all go to the father of the community,* must be punished forty days in penance, unless he himself says *I am sorry for what I said.*

Let him who does not ask pardon when corrected do penance with a special fast. He who has visited other brethren in their cells without asking leave, let him do penance likewise; or if he has gone to the kitchen after nones, with a special fast; or if he has gone outside the wall, that is, outside the bounds of the monastery, without asking, with an imposition. Youths who are assigned a period for not speaking to each other, if they have transgressed it, with three special fasts. And if anyone has commanded what they are not allowed, let them say, *You know that we are not allowed;* and if the other insists on his command, let him be condemned to three special fasts, but let them say, *We do what you say,* so that the good of obedience may be preserved. But they must particularly beware, that just as they do not speak together amongst themselves, so they do not confer either through the lips of another brother. But if they have transgressed this knowingly, let them do penance in the same way as if they had spoken amongst themselves....

He who utters an idle word, to be condemned to silence for the two following hours, or to twelve blows.

Let brethren doing penance, however hard and dirty the work they do, not wash their heads except on the Lord's day, that is, the eighth, but if not, on every fifteenth day; or certainly, on account of the growth of flowing locks, let each employ the judgement of his senior in washing. If the immediate superior is made aware of minor penances at table, let him impose them there, and let no more than twenty-five blows be given at one time.

Brethren doing penance, and those who need a penance of psalms—that is, one for whom it has been necessary that he should chant further psalms on account of a night dream, because of a devilish delusion, or because of the nature of his dream—should, when they need a penance of psalms, chant, some thirty, some twenty-four psalms in order, some fifteen, others twelve; and thus these persons, as penitents, bend the knee (even) on the Lord's night and in the season of Easter-tide.

But all the brethren together, every day and night at the time of prayers, on the ending of all psalms, should uniformly bend their knees in prayer, if bodily weakness does not prevent it, saying in silence, *O God make*

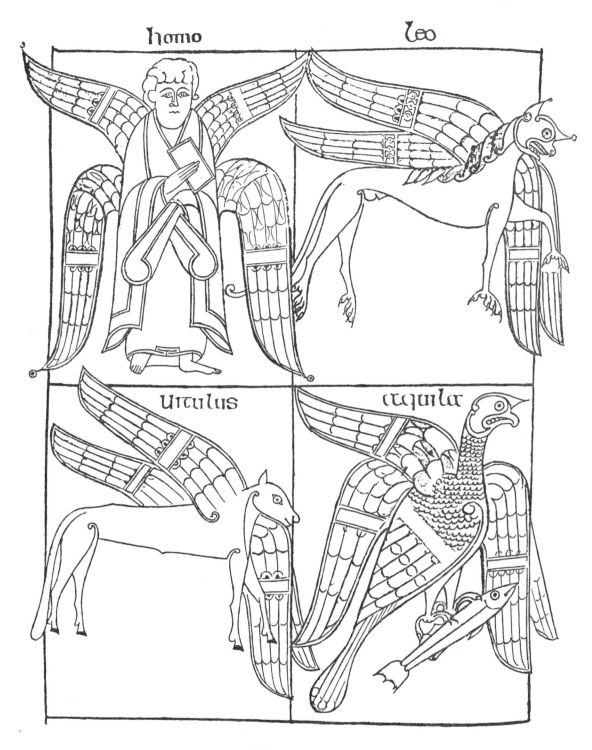

Symbols of the Four Evangelists in the Book of Armagh.

speed to save me, O Lord make haste to help me (Psalm 69.2). And after they have chanted this verse silently thrice in prayer, let them rise uniformly from their bending in prayer, except on the Lord's Days and from the first day of holy Easter up to the fiftieth day, on which, while they bow themselves slightly in time of psalmody, let them without bending their knees pray carefully to the Lord.

39

For all its precious detail this picture is one-sided. It dwells—inevitably—on the trespasses of monks and their expiation by various forms of penance. There are other sources from which we can learn something about the daily life of Irish monks, about their prayer and work, their mortifications and their joys. This picture must be pieced together from details which are scattered over the Lives of Irish saints. Although most of these date from the twelfth century or later, they are based on earlier accounts, and even if this earlier stratum is, as a rule, not contemporary with the saint, it usually gives valuable information about his community at the time when those accounts were written. Of exceptional historical value is the Life of St. Columcille which was composed by one of his successors at Iona, Adamnán (d. 704), between the years 680 and 690. Less than a hundred years had passed since the saint had died in the very same place where Adamnán wrote. His memory was still fresh in the community, and the monks would have been living much the same sort of life as in the founder's time. In this case it is impossible to quote a continuous text: Adamnán gives many interesting details *en passant* which must be put together in a historical synthesis.

The monks formed a community in the fullest meaning of the word. The monastic community was self-supporting, and its internal life was governed by the principles of perfect mutual love, common property without exception, and strict obedience, which the monk owed not only to his abbot but also to his seniors in the monastery. Chastity, humility, and the mortification of body and will, being essential parts of monastic life, were practised rigorously. The obligation of silence was not enforced as strictly as elsewhere, but the monks were not allowed to indulge in idle talk. About the practice of psalmody at Iona we know nothing in detail; it may be assumed, however, that it did not differ greatly from the practice of other monasteries. Liturgy in Ireland, as in the ancient Church generally, centred upon the celebration of Sunday. Only a few other days were celebrated liturgically: the principal feasts of the ecclesiastical year and the memorial days *(natales)* of a small number of saints. On the vigil of Sunday the Office lasted the whole night. It began with vespers *(vespertinalis missa)* on Saturday and ended with high mass *(missarum sollemnia)* after nones on Sunday. Wednesday and Friday were fast days; on these days no food was taken before the ninth hour. During Lent the fast was not broken until sunset. This rigorous fast was sometimes lightened by special dispensation—on the arrival of a guest, for example, the abbot would give permission for an earlier meal. The strict life was slightly mitigated during the fifty days between Easter and Pentecost.

The monks wore the "Celtic" tonsure, which extended "from ear to ear", as is said in general of the "second order of Irish saints". The front only of the head was shaved, but the remainder of the hair was allowed to grow. This tonsure is seen, for example, in the drawing of the Man (one of the symbols of the evangelists) in the Book of Durrow. The monk's dress consisted of an undergarment *(tunica)*, which was of heavier material during the winter, and a cowl *(cuculla)*. When working out of doors or travelling, the monks wore sandals. Their beds were furnished with straw mattresses which, it seems, were covered with hides. A pious custom not mentioned by Adamnán, but known from other monastic writers, was the carrying on one's body of a blessed host in a little box *(chrysmal)*; its loss had to be atoned for by severe penance.

The most important hours of the monastic day were those set aside for common prayer. The remainder was devoted to work and study. Columba himself was never seen idle: he would either pray or read or write,

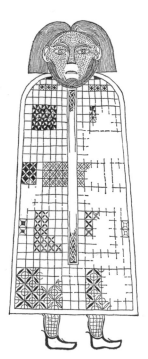

The Man (symbol of an evangelist) in the Book of Durrow.

or even take his share in the manual work of the brethren. That the abbot did not consider himself exempt from working for the material needs of his community is evident from the Lives of some Irish abbots, who are said to have joined their monks in manual labour whenever their responsibilities would allow them to do so.

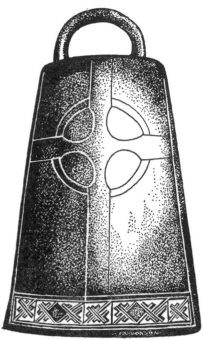

Monastic bell of bronze with engraved ornament, from Lough Lene Castle, Co. Westmeath. Royal Irish Academy, Dublin.

Columba, who was a member of the order of learned poets *(filid)*, brought to the monastery his zeal for study. As has been said, the Psalter known as the *Cathach* is believed to have been a work of his pen. From the colophon in the Book of Durrow we conclude that this Gospel book also was copied from a manuscript written in Columba's own hand. Iona evidently had a scriptorium of considerable importance. Even the Book of Kells was possibly written there, and taken to Kells at the beginning of the ninth century in order to rescue it from the Vikings. Iona is certainly the home of the earliest manuscript of Adamnán's Life of St. Columba, written by the calligrapher Dorbbéne, who was abbot in 713.

The novice was, as a matter of course, taught to write. As in antiquity, he wrote his exercises on waxed tablets, using a stylus for writing. Such tablets were also used for notes, jottings, and drafts of literary works. Adamnán tells us that he used *tabulae* for taking down Bishop Arculf's account of the Holy Places. (Arculf, a bishop of Gaul, had made a pilgrimage to the Holy Land; on his return journey a storm had driven his vessel off-route and had forced him to land at Iona, where he enjoyed the hospitality of the abbot, Adamnán, and his community. They listened eagerly to the pilgrim's stories; Adamnán took notes all the time, and out of these later composed his three books *De Locis Sanctis*.) Often several tablets were united so as to form a small book *(codicillus)*; two such books were found in Irish bogs and are now exhibited in the National Museum in Dublin. The primer of the young monk would seem to have been the Psalter. If hagiographers of later times can be believed, this tradition started with St. Patrick, who is said to have written *abgitoria (abecedaria*, probably the text of Psalm 118* or of some other abecedarian psalm) for some of his converts. One of the Dublin bog-books also contains psalm-texts.

* In the vulgate num- bering; Psalm 119 in the Hebrew and English Psalters.

Winged lion
(symbol of Mark) in
the Book of Armagh.
Opposite: The upper
part of page 3 of a
copy of Priscian's
Latin Grammar
written in Irish
minuscule, c. 850.

Although many a monk must have been capable of copying a text for practical use, few would have been skilled enough for the execution of those beautiful books, intended for liturgical or semi-liturgical use, which were the pride of a community. For these tasks scribes had to be specially trained. *Scriba*, as has been remarked, was a title of honour. The Irish script could not have been brought to perfection in such a short time without a carefully nurtured tradition of calligraphy.

The monk was also supposed to study privately in his cell. He had, first of all, to become thoroughly familiar with Sacred Scripture, with the Old as well as with the New Testament, and to understand its spiritual meaning. For this purpose he had to study the commentaries of the Fathers. As a more convenient aid to Biblical studies, excerpts from patristic commentaries were made as early as the seventh century, and these were pieced together in *catena*-like fashion with a view to providing comprehensive commentaries on the whole Bible. A "Biblical encyclopedia" of this kind, which dates from the end of the eighth century, is preserved in several manuscripts. For edification the monk would read Lives of the saints, for example the Life of St. Martin of Tours by Sulpicius Severus, or the Lives of the Fathers of the Egyptian desert. Favourite reading matter was also the Conferences (*Collationes*) and Instructions of Cassian. In addition, the library at Iona contained some texts which were not so common, for example the so-called Hegesippus, a Christian Latin re-writing of Josephus's *Jewish Wars*, and the Gospel Harmony in hexameters by Juvencus. Both works are quoted by Adamnán.

Such studies could not be undertaken without preparation. The elementary disciplines, called the Arts (*Artes*), had been integrated into a system of "liberal education" in late antiquity, and this system was taken over by the medieval schools. The fundamental discipline was (Latin) grammar. One of the standard books on Latin grammar, that of Priscian (c. 500), is known from several Irish manuscripts of the ninth century, which are now in Leyden and Saint Gall. Numerous glosses in Old Irish, which make these manuscripts most valuable to Celtic philologists, show how thoroughly this textbook was studied in the Irish schools. Adamnán has with some probability been suggested as the author of a commentary on Virgil, the *Scholia Bernensia*. Of Adamnán's rhetorical training there is ample evidence in his writings, and he was not the only Irish author to master this art. The higher

Opposite:
Centre-piece of fol.
2 V of the Lindisfarne
Gospels c. 720.

studies of dialectics and science were, as far as our evidence goes, rather neglected; this is certainly true of the earlier period. In the late eighth and the ninth centuries, and especially on the Continent, some Irishmen distinguished themselves in these fields, as did Virgil of Salzburg, Dicuil, and John Scottus.

In the early ninth century, too, falls the famous Old Irish poem, written by a monk of Reichenau on Lake Constance, in which the author introduces the faithful companion of his studies, the white cat Pangur. Both go hunting without disturbing one another: Pangur pursues mice, the scholar knowledge; both are sometimes successful in their endeavours, and rejoice at their success; both love their quiet occupations and have mastered them by daily practice.

The poem on the Cat Pangur in a Reichenau MS now at St. Paul in Carinthia.

The material needs of a self-supporting community of any size, even if its members were bound to observe the most frugal and ascetic life, must have made considerable demands on all able-bodied brethren; even special skills were often required. Adamnán refers to *fratres operarii* as a distinct category of monks at Iona. These "working brethren" apparently had some special training as farmers and craftsmen, and would normally be entrusted with most of the work in the fields and pastures, in the stables, in the mill and kitchen. Some would have been employed also as smiths, leather-workers, masons, and carpenters. They were probably exempt from the common chanting of the Office. Their work was regulated either by the abbot in person or by a deputy (*praepositus, oeconomus*). Later Lives of saints often depict these *oeconomi* as harsh and tyrannical, as persons who put the obedience of those under their authority to almost inhuman tests. On some icy winter's day Columba saw in a vision that Laisrén, his deputy in far-off Durrow, was working his monks beyond their strength at the erection of some building, and was saddened. In the same moment, however, Laisrén received a spiritual message, which prompted him to allow the monks to rest and to grant them an extra meal; after that day he never sent them out again to work in the open air in rough weather.

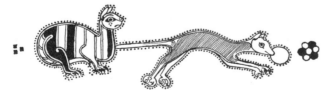

Frieze of cats in the Book of Kells.

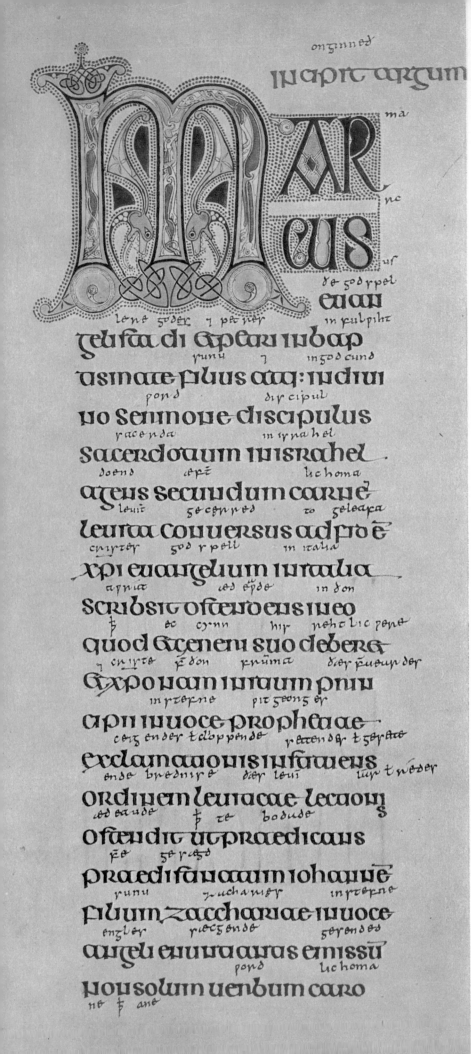

A column of fol. 90 R of the Lindisfarne Gospels, beginning with the enlarged word MARCUS. Between the lines of the Latin text an Anglo-Saxon translation was inserted in the 10th century.

Iona being an island, sailing was a necessity. The monastery had at its disposal several harbours and a number of boats of varying size and construction. There was regular traffic with the Scottish mainland, but communications with the home country would also have been fairly regular, because the government of the widespread net of monasteries founded by Columba required frequent contact between the individual houses and their monastic centre. In the circumstances it is not surprising that there are few Lives of saints, apart from the Life of St. Brendan, in which references to sailing are more numerous than in that of St. Columba.

Whether on the seashore or inland, Irish monks were keen fishermen. As Irish monastic rules allowed the use of meat only on rare occasions, fish was probably the most nourishing food in the monk's ordinary diet. It could be obtained almost everywhere easily and plentifully. The place which fish and fishing had in the monk's daily life explains partly why the fish makes such frequent appearances as an ornament in the initials of Irish manuscripts. We must not forget, however, that the fish had, since ancient times, been a symbol of Christ and of the Church.

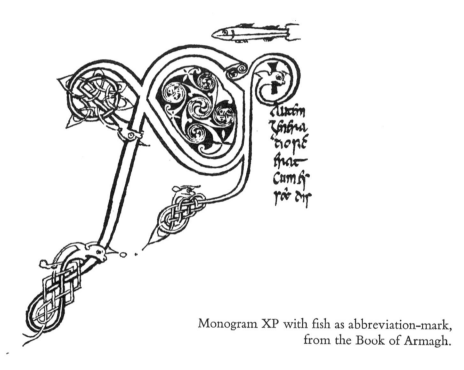

Monogram XP with fish as abbreviation-mark,
from the Book of Armagh.

One of the most attractive features of the early Irish monasteries was the great importance attached to the practice of hospitality. Here a monastic virtue and a traditional Irish one meet. Any stranger was sincerely welcomed; he could be sure of being introduced to the abbot in due course and receiving his kiss of peace. If a guest was expected, the brethren would go down to the harbour to receive him, and then lead him in procession to their church. After a prayer of thanksgiving for the happily completed journey, the guest was led to his quarters and was well looked after. His feet were washed, and he was given every comfort the monastery was able to provide. If he arrived on a Wednesday or Friday, the fast was shortened and better and richer food was served. In an episode in the Life of St. Columba the hospitality of Iona is extended even to a bird:

At one time, while the saint was living in the island of Io, he called in one of the brothers, and thus addressed him: "On the third day from this that dawns, you must watch in the western part of this island, sitting above the sea-shore; for after the ninth hour of the day a guest will arrive from the northern region of Ireland, very tired and weary, a crane that has been tossed by winds through long circuits of the air. And with its strength almost exhausted it will fall near you and lie upon the shore. You will take heed to lift it tenderly, and carry it to the house near by; and, having taken it in as a guest there you will wait upon it for three days and nights, and feed it with anxious care. And afterwards, at the end of the three days, revived and not wishing to be longer in pilgrimage with us, it will return with fully recovered strength to the sweet district of Ireland from which at first it came. I commend it to you thus earnestly, for this reason, that it comes from the district of our fathers."

The brother obeyed; and on the third day, after the ninth hour, as he had been bidden, he awaited the coming of the foreknown guest. When it arrived, he lifted it from the shore where it had fallen; in its weakness, he carried it to the lodging; in its hunger, he fed it. When he returned to the monastery in the evening, the saint, not questioning but affirming, said to him: "God bless you, my son, because you have tended well the pilgrim guest; which will not remain in pilgrimage, but after three days will return home."

This, precisely as the saint foretold, the event also proved to be true. After being a guest for three days, it first rose from the ground in the presence of its host that had cared for it, and flew to a height; and then, after studying the way for a while in the air, crossed the expanse of ocean, and in calm weather took its way back to Ireland, in a straight line of flight.

Large monasteries, for example Iona and Lismore, had special guest houses *(hospitia)*. This tradition was transplanted to the Continent in the course of the Irish expansion during the seventh century. Irish monks built and ran hostels for pilgrims, and in particular for pilgrims to Rome.

The monasteries were the spiritual centres of the country. Big churches like that of Kildare, which were designed for large congregations, testify to the fact that a monastery was the religious centre of an entire district. Irish monasteries, however, were more closely connected with the neighbouring population than were monasteries elsewhere. It was in the nature of early Irish society that a monastery should have close links with its founder's family and with the tribal kingdom *(tuath)* in which it was

Ornamental beasts from the Book of Kells.

48

situated. The abbacy of a monastery was almost regularly held by a member of the family to which its founder had belonged. In many places succession within a family was regarded almost as being by right, and the monastery, especially if, in course of time, it had grown rich in treasures and landed property, was considered to belong to the family of the founder. The dangers inherent in this system are obvious; they made themselves felt most acutely in the wealthy plain of Leinster. Even at Iona, where the true monastic spirit was preserved for many generations, the abbots, with few exceptions, were chosen from the family of St. Columba, although there was no regular succession. Another link between a *tuath* and its monasteries was the custom of many families to give one son in each generation to "their" monastery—as a sort of tithe, according to the spirit of the Mosaic Law.

That the monasteries had their share also in pastoral work is best seen in their contribution to the administration of penance. It was in Ireland that the ancient Christian system of public penance was first replaced by private confession and private penance, consisting of prayers and works of mortification enjoined on the penitent by the confessor. This form of penance has its roots in the penitential practice of primitive monasticism, but it became a system only in the monasteries of Wales and Ireland. The Rule and the Penitential of St. Columbanus demand of the monk that he should regularly confess not only sinful deeds but also, after a careful examination of conscience, every sinful thought. Starting with the monasteries, this new penance soon found its way also to the laity. The confessor (Irish *anmchara*, "soul-friend") begins to assume the role of spiritual director and counsellor. St. Comgall is credited with the saying: "A man without a soul-friend is like a body without its head."

Most of the Penitentials that have been preserved set forth separately penances for monks or clerics and penances for lay people. In the Penitential of Columbanus these two sets of provisions are kept most clearly distinct. In the other Penitentials the penitent's status is not the basis for classification; in respect of each sin penances are laid down for religious and for laymen, and they differ merely in their duration. These details show clearly that the Irish Penitentials are not "mirrors" for penitents but guides for confessors. Penances vary both in length and in severity according to the nature of the sin, the frequency and persistence in committing it, the state or rank of the sinner, and his mental disposition. The penances consist mainly in prayer, fasting, and (in the case of lay penitents) alms-giving. Alms were often accepted as a substitute for other penances, especially if the penitent was not in good health, or if the penance prescribed would have been of long duration. The substitution of alms for other forms of penance has a parallel in Old Irish Law; even the amount of the "equivalent" penance is measured according to the same unit—the value of a female slave—as is the legal "price" of a blow or a murder.

The earliest Penitential of any length was compiled by a certain Vennia(n)us or Vinnianus, possibly St. Finnian of Clonard; a less likely candidate for its authorship is the younger Finnian of Moville. An indirect argument for the authorship of Finnian of Clonard is the fact that the Penitential of St. Columbanus is modelled on that of "Vinnian", and that Columbanus's monastic teachers, Sinell and Comgall, were both pupils of Finnian of Clonard. Of great importance was the Penitential of Cummaine Fota (Cumianus Longus, Cummean), who died in 662. It is arranged according to the eight "capital sins" as formulated by Cassian: greed, fornication, avarice, anger, despondency, sloth, vanity, pride. This framework, together with much of the actual contents of Cummean's Penitential, was taken over by the authors of Penitentials in the Frankish Church during the eighth century. The Penitentials of Columbanus and Cummean were widely used on the Continent, and exercised great influence on penitential literature and on the development of penitential discipline during the Middle Ages.

Something of the form and spirit of the Irish Penitentials may be learned from the following extracts from the Penitential of "Vinnian":

In the name of the Father and of the Son and of the Holy Ghost.

1. *If anyone has sinned by thought in his heart and immediately repents, he shall beat his breast and seek pardon from God and make satisfaction, and (so) be whole.*

2. *But if he frequently entertains (evil) thoughts and hesitates to act on them, whether he has mastered them or been mastered by them, he shall seek help from God by prayer and fasting day and night until the evil thought departs and he is whole.*

3. *If, however, he has thought evil and intended to do it and has not been able to do it, since opportunity has failed him, it is the same sin but not the same penance; for example, if he intended fornication or murder, he has, by his intention, already committed the sin in his heart which he did not complete by a deed; but if he quickly does penance, he can be helped. His penance is this: half a year he shall do penance on an allowance of bread and water, and he shall abstain from wine and meat for a whole year.*

4. *If anyone has sinned in word by inadvertence and immediately repented, and has not said any such thing of set purpose, he ought to submit to penance, but he shall keep (only) one special fast; but thereafter let him be on his guard throughout his life, lest he commit further sin.*

5. *If one of the clerics or ministers of God makes strife, he shall do penance for a period of seven days with bread and water and salt, and seek pardon from God and his neighbour, with full confession and humility; and thus can he be reconciled to God and his neighbour.*

6. *If anyone has decided on a scandalous deed and plotted in his heart to strike or kill his neighbour, if (the offender) is a cleric, he shall do penance for half a year with an allowance of bread and water and for a whole year abstain from wine and meat, and thus he will be reconciled to the altar; 7. but if he is a layman, he shall do penance for a period of seven days; since he is a man of this world, his guilt is lighter in this world and his reward less in the world to come.*

8. *But if he is a cleric and strikes his brother or his neighbour or sheds blood, it is the same as if he had killed him, but the penance is not the same: he shall do penance with bread and water and salt and be deprived of his clerical office for an entire year, and he must pray with weeping and tears, that he may obtain mercy of God, since Scripture says: Whosoever hateth his brother is a murderer; how much more he who strikes him. 9. But if he is a layman, he shall do penance forty days and give some money to him whom he has struck, according as some priest or arbiter determines. A cleric, however, ought not to give money to either man or woman.*

Ornamental beasts from the Book of Kells.

10. *But if one who is a cleric falls miserably through fornication and loses his crown, if it happens once (only) and it is concealed from men but known before God, he shall do penance for an entire year with an allowance of bread and water and for two years abstain from wine and meat, but he shall not lose his clerical office. For, we say, sins can be absolved in secret by penance and by very diligent devotion of heart and body. 11. If, however, they have long been in the habit of sin and it has not come to the notice of men, he shall do penance for three years with bread and water and lose his clerical office, and for three years more he shall abstain from wine and meat, since it is not a smaller thing to sin before God than before men.*

12. But if one of the clerical order falls to the depths of ruin and begets a son and kills him, great is the crime of fornication with homicide, but it can be expiated through penance and God's mercy. He shall do penance three years with an allowance of bread and water, in weeping and tears, and prayers by day and night, and shall implore the mercy of the Lord, if he may perchance have remission of sins; and he shall abstain for three more years from wine and meat, deprived of his clerical office, and for the forty-day periods in the last three years he shall fast with bread and water; and (he shall) be an exile from his own country, until a period of seven years is completed, and so by the judgement of a bishop or a priest he shall be restored to his office.

13. If, however, he has not killed the child, the sin is less, but the penance is the same.

14. But if one of the clerical order is on familiar terms with any woman and he has himself done no evil with her, neither by cohabiting nor by lascivious embraces, this is his penance: For such time as he has her he shall withdraw from the communion of the altar and do penance for forty days and nights with bread and water and tear out of his heart his fellowship with the woman, and so be restored to the altar....

16. If any cleric lusts after a virgin or any woman in his heart but does not speak with his lips, if he sins thus but once he ought to do penance for seven days with an allowance of bread and water. 17. But if he continually lusts and is unable to indulge his desire, since the woman does not admit him or since he is ashamed to speak, still he has committed adultery with her in his heart—yet it is in his heart, and not in his body; it is the same sin whether in the heart or in the body, yet the penance is not the same. This is his penance: let him do penance for forty days with bread and water.

18. If any cleric or woman who practises magic have led astray anyone by their magic, it is a monstrous sin, but it can be expiated by penance. (Such an offender) shall do penance for six years, three years on an allowance of bread and water, and during the remaining three years he shall abstain from wine and meat. 19. If, however, such a person has not led astray anyone but has given (a potion) for the sake of wanton love to someone, he shall do penance for an entire year on an allowance of bread and water.

20. If a woman by her magic destroys the child she has conceived of somebody, she shall do penance for half a year with an allowance of bread and water, and abstain for two years from wine and meat and fast for the six forty-day periods with bread and water.

21. But if, as we have said, she bears a child and her sin is manifest, she shall do penance for six years with bread and water, as is the judgement in the case of a cleric, and in the seventh year she shall be joined to the altar, and then we say her crown can be restored and she may don a white robe and be pronounced a virgin. So a cleric who has fallen ought likewise to receive the clerical office in the seventh year after the labour of penance, as saith Scripture: Seven times a just man falleth and ariseth, that is, after seven years of penance he who fell can be called "just" and in the eighth year evil shall not lay hold on him, but for the remainder (of his life) let him preserve carefully lest he fall, since, as Solomon saith, as a dog returning to his vomit becomes odious, so is he who through his own negligence reverts to his sin.

22. If one has sworn a false oath, great is the crime; it can hardly, if at all, be expiated, but none the less it is better to do penance and not to despair: for great is the mercy of God. This is his penance: first, he must never in his life take an oath, since a man who swears much will not be justified and the scourge shall not depart from his house, that is, whatever good he has done will perish, and in future punishment will never leave his tent; but

in the present time one must, by the medicine of immediate penance, prevent perpetual pains in the future, and do penance for seven years and for the rest of one's life do right, not take oaths, and set free a maid-servant or man-servant or give the value of one to the poor and needy.

23. If any cleric commits murder and strikes down his neighbour and he is dead, he must become an exile from his country for ten years and do penance seven years in another city, three years of this time on an allowance of bread and water and salt, and for four years he shall abstain from wine and meat, and fast during the forty-day periods on an allowance of bread and water and salt; and having thus completed the ten years, if he has done well and is approved by testimonial of the abbot or priest to whom he was committed, he shall be received into his own country and make satisfaction to the friends of him whom he slew, and compensate his father and mother, if they are still in the flesh, by filial piety and obedience and say: "Lo, I am in the place of your son; I will do for you whatever you tell me." But if he does not fulfil his obligation he shall not be received back forever.

24. But if he kills him suddenly and not from hatred—the two having formerly been friends—but by the prompting of the devil ensnaring him, he shall do penance for three years on an allowance of bread and water, and for three more years he shall abstain from wine and meat, and not (stay) in his own country.

25. If a cleric commits theft once or twice, that is, steals his neighbour's sheep or hog or any animal, he shall do penance an entire year on an allowance of bread and water and shall restore fourfold to his neighbour. 26. If, however, he does it, not once or twice, but of long habit, he shall do penance for three years, the first year on an allowance of bread and water and salt, and for the other two he shall abstain from wine and meat.

27. If anyone is a cleric of the rank of a deacon or of any rank, and if he formerly was a layman, and if he lives with his sons and daughters and with his mate and if he returns to carnal desire and begets a son with his own mate, as he might say, let him know that he has fallen to the depths of ruin and ought to rise; his sin is not less than it would be if he had been a cleric from his youth and sinned with a strange girl, since they have sinned after their vow and after they were consecrated to God, and then they have made their vow void. They shall do penance for three years on an allowance of bread and water and shall abstain for three years more from wine and meat, and they shall not do penance together, but separately, and then in the seventh year they shall be joined to the altar and shall receive their rank.

28. But if a cleric is covetous, this is a great offence, for covetousness is declared idolatry, but it is corrected by liberality and alms and humility. This is the penance for his offence, that he cure and correct contraries by contraries....

30. He who despoils monasteries, falsely saying that he is collecting money for the redemption of captives, shall do penance for one year with bread and water, and all that he has gathered he shall give to the poor, and for two years he shall do penance without wine and meat.

31. But if he does not repent he is to be excommunicated and be anathema to all Christians; he shall be driven from the bounds of his country and beaten with rods until he is converted—if he has compunction....

34. If any man or woman is nigh unto death, although he (or she) has been a sinner, and asks for the communion of Christ we say that it is not to be denied to such a person if that person promise God to take the vow, and do well and be received by Him. If he is restored to this world, let him fulfil that which he has vowed to God; but if he does not fulfil the vow which he has vowed to God, (the consequences) will be on his own head, and we will not refuse what we owe to him: we are not to cease to snatch prey from the mouth of the lion or the dragon, that is of the devil, who ceases not to snatch at the prey of our souls, even though we may have to follow up and strive (for his soul) at the very end of a man's life.

35. If one of the laity is converted from his evil-doing unto the Lord, and if he has wrought every evil deed, by committing fornication, that is, and shedding blood, he shall do penance for three years and go unarmed except for a staff in his hand, and shall not live with his wife, but in the first year he shall fast on an allowance of bread and water and salt and not live with his wife; after a penance of three years he shall give money for the redemption of his soul and the fruit of his penance into the hand of the priest and make a feast for the servants of God, and in the feast (his penance) shall be ended and he shall be received to communion; he may then resume relations with his wife after his entire and complete penance, and if it is so decided he shall be joined to the altar.

36. If any layman defiles his neighbour's wife or virgin daughter, he shall do penance for an entire year on an allowance of bread and water, and he shall not have intercourse with his own wife, and after a year of penance he shall be received to communion, and shall give alms for his soul; and so long as he is in this body, he shall not go in to commit fornication again with a strange woman; or if (he defiles) a virgin, two years shall be his penance: the first with bread and water, in the other (year) he shall fast during the forty-day periods and abstain from wine and meat; and he shall give alms to the poor and the fruit of his penitence into the hands of his priest.

37. If any layman has defiled a vowed virgin and she has lost her crown and he has begotten a child by her, let such a layman do penance for three years; in the first year he shall go on an allowance of bread and water and unarmed and shall not have intercourse with his own wife, and for two years he shall abstain from wine and meat and shall not have intercourse with his wife. 38. If, however, he does not beget a child of her, but nevertheless has defiled the virgin, he shall do penance for an entire year and a half, an entire year on an allowance of bread and water, and for half a year he shall abstain from wine and meat, and he shall not have intercourse with his wife until his penance is completed.

39. If any layman with a wife of his own has intercourse with his female slave, the procedure is this: the female slave is to be sold, and he himself shall not have intercourse with his own wife for an entire year. 40. But if he begets by this female slave one, two, or three children, he is to set her free, and if he wishes to sell her it shall not be permitted to him, but they shall be separated from each other, and he shall do penance an entire year on an allowance of bread and water; and he shall have no further intercourse with his concubine but be joined to his own wife.

41. If anyone has a barren wife, he shall not turn away his wife because of her barrenness, but this is what shall be done: they shall both dwell in continence, and blessed they are if they persevere in chastity of body until God pronounces a true and just judgement upon them. For I believe that if they be as Abraham and Sarah were, or Isaac and Rebecca, or Anna the mother of Samuel, or Elizabeth the mother of John, it will come out well for them at the last. For the Apostle saith: And let those that have wives be as if they had none. For the fashion of this world passeth away. But if we remain faithful in that which God hath given, whether it be prosperity or adversity, we shall always receive with joy the glory of God....

43. *If a man's wife commits fornication and cohabits with another man, he ought not to take another wife while his first wife is alive, (44) in the hope that, perchance, she be converted to penance, and it is becoming to take her back, if she fully and freely seeks this; but he shall not give her a dowry, and she shall go into service to her former husband as long as he is in the body: she shall make amends in the place of a male or a female slave, in all loyalty and subjection. 45. So also a woman, if she has been sent away by her husband, must not mate with another man so long as her former husband is in the body, but should wait for him, unmarried, in all patience and chastity, in the hope that God may perchance put penance in the heart of her husband. But the penance of these persons is this—that is, of a man or woman who has committed fornication: they shall do penance for an entire year on an allowance of bread and water separately and shall not sleep in the same bed.*

46. *We prescribe and exhort that there be continence in marriage, since marriage without continence is not lawful, but sin, and (marriage), by the authority of God, is permitted not for lust but for the sake of children, as it is written, And they shall be two in one flesh, that is, in unity of the flesh for the generation of children, not for the lustful concupiscence of the flesh. Married people, then, should mutually abstain during the three forty-day periods in each single year, by consent for the time being, that they may be able to have time for prayer for the salvation of their souls; and on Sunday night or Saturday night they shall mutually abstain; and after the wife has conceived he shall not have intercourse with her until she has borne her child, and they shall come together again for this purpose, as saith the Apostle. But if they shall fulfil this instruction, then they are worthy of the Lord's body, if by good works they fulfil matrimony, that is, with alms and by fulfilling the commands of God and expelling their faults, and in the life to come they shall reign with Christ, with holy Abraham, Isaac, Jacob, Job, Noah, all the saints; and there they shall receive the thirtyfold fruit which the Saviour in the Gospel, in his account (of rewards), has set aside for married people.*

47. *If the child of anyone departs without baptism and was lost through negligence, great is the crime of occasioning the loss of a soul, but its expiation through penance is possible, since there is no crime which cannot be expiated through penance so long as we are in this body; the parents shall do penance for an entire year with bread and water and not sleep in the same bed...*

(Postscript:) THANKS BE TO GOD

These few things concerning the remedies of penance, my dearly beloved brethren, according to the pronouncement of Scripture and to the opinion of some very learned men, I have tried to write down, compelled by love of you, beyond my ability and authority. There are still other authoritative decisions concerning either the remedies or the several kinds of those (things?) who (or: that?) are to be cured, which now a concern for brevity, or the situation of the place, or the poverty of my talent does not permit me to set down. But if any diligent searcher of divine reading should for himself find out more, or bring forth and write down better things, we, too, shall agree and follow him.

Here ends the little work which Finnian adapted for the sons of his bowels, out of affection and in the interest of religion, overflowing with the waters of the Scriptures, in order that by all men evil deeds might be destroyed.

Genealogy of Christ, fol. 201 R
of the Book of Kells.

As early as the seventh century the strict observance of the rule began, here and there, to give way to a more worldly spirit, and this became common during the eighth. Such monastic "cities" as Glendalough, Kildare, Bangor, Clonmacnoise had greatly increased their property by pious donations and enjoyed the patronage of kings and nobles. In such circumstances learning and the arts would flourish, but the wealth on which these pursuits could thrive was also a danger. The ruling class and in particular the royal "clan" of a *tuath* was likely to take a keen interest in "their" monasteries from the economic point of view. Abbots frequently succeeded one another according to the laws of secular hereditary succession; even a layman could become *coarb* ("heir") of the founder. Men of this kind would take little interest in the spiritual and intellectual life of their community, but would have a keen eye on the property of the monastery and on the revenue from its *paruchia*. The latter consisted mainly in a tribute or tithe, called the "law" *(lex,* Irish *cáin)* of the founder, which was levied periodically throughout the territory belonging to the monastery. As the high king *(árd-rí)* would tour the territories of his vassal kings and levy tribute in person, so the monks made regular circuits of the monastic *paruchia*, carrying with them the relics of their founder, who, as it were, also demanded his dues in person. Another source of income was the offerings of pilgrims. In order to attract as many pilgrims as possible the Lives of saints who had founded monasteries were sometimes rewritten in a mercenary spirit. The miraculous element, which in the earlier Lives had been balanced by a strong emphasis on ascetical rigour, became predominant. In order to recommend the invocation of a certain saint as a sure remedy in every possible emergency these hagiographers invented without scruple all sorts of extravagant miracle stories, some even of a rather doubtful morality, for example the disappearance of illegitimate pregnancy at the saint's intercession. Small wonder that monastic discipline was on the decline.

Those who strove earnestly for the ascetical life often preferred to retire from a community that had grown lax. Their ties with the monastery were purely spiritual; their actual lives were lived in solitude (though near the monastery) and in a strictly ascetical manner. How serious these men were in their retreat from worldliness, be it even the worldliness of a wealthy monastery, is proved by religious poems such as the "Song of the Hermit", which dates from the ninth century:

HERMITS

Alone in my little cell,
no paltry man for company—
this were my chosen pilgrimage
before trysting with death.

A little secret hidden place
for forgiveness of sin
so that to holy heaven I bear
a clear untarnished mind.

To train and sanctify the flesh,
manfully trample on it,
and with the tears of feeble eyes
to wash out all desires.

Withered and weak desire,
rejected the paltry world,
mind gleaming white and vigorous—
so may I come to God.

Let bitter wailing reach
up to yon heaven of clouds;
be sins confessed in piety
with free and copious tears.

Be cold my bed and full of fear
like where a doomed captive lies,
be short my sleep and hazardous,
with cries to God at every hour.

My food, all the things I have,
are a longed for captivity;
I warrant that what I eat
will rouse no wrong proclivities.

Bread stale and weighed
(bow low the head in reverence)
and be the drink I drink
clear water from the mountain stream.

Little food, and tasteless too,
and the mind but set on learning;
farewell to strife and company,
welcome calm and quiet mind.

A washed and holy soul
were a lovely garment,
with withered shrunken cheeks,
skin tight-stretched and tough.

And Christ, God's son, to visit me,
my creator, my king—
and then my mind to seek him out
in the kingdom where He lives.

And be the earth that covers me
hallowed earth of monastery,
a tiny place with gleaming tombs,
I lying there alone.

Ornamental beasts from the Book of Kells.

Another poem of the ninth century paints the life of a hermit with brighter colours, and is one of the most attractive specimens of Celtic nature poetry. It is a (fictitious) dialogue between King Gúaire of Connacht (died c. 663) and his half-brother, the hermit Marbán.

I have a bothy in the wood—
none knows it save the Lord, my God;
one wall an ash, the other hazel,
and a great fern makes the door.

The doorposts are made of heather,
the lintel of honeysuckle;
and wild forest all around
yields mast for well-fed swine.

This size my hut: the smallest thing,
homestead amid well-trod paths;
a woman (but blackbird clothed and seeming)
warbles sweetly from its gable.

. . .

This little secret humble place
holds tenure of the teeming woods;
maybe you will come to see?—
but alone I live quite happy.

Smooth the tresses *of yew-green yew-trees,*
 glorious portent;
place delicious *with great green oakwoods*
 increasing blessing.

Tree of apples, *huge and magic,*
 great its graces;
crop in fistfulls *from clustered hazel,*
 green and branching.

Sparkling wells *and water-torrents,*
 best for drinking;
green privet there *and bird-cherry*
 and yew-berries.

Resting there *are herded swine,*
 goats and piglings;
wild swine too, *deer and doe,*
 speckled badgers.

Great woodland bands   troop like fairies
    to my bothy;
and great delight   when timid foxes
    show their faces.

.   .   .

Eggs in clutches,   and God gives mast,
    honey, heath-pease;
sweet the apples   and the berries
    of bog and heather.

.   .   .

A cup of mead   from noble hazel,
    swift the service;
acorns brown,   bramble tresses,
    their good berries.

And in summer   pleasant mantle
    of tasty savour:
marjoram, earth-nuts,   and the tresses
    of the streamlet.

Pigeons cooing,   breasts a-gleaming,
    beloved flutter;
on my house-top   constant music,
    song of thrushes.

Bees and chafers,   gentle humming
    and soft crooning;
and wild geese come,   the black and grey ones,
    before All Hallows.

.   .   .

Then come dear white ones,   herons, sea-gulls
    sea-chant hearing;
no harsh music   when grouse is calling
    from russet heather.

The sound of wind   in branching trees,
    day grey and cloudy;
stream in torrent,   swans a-singing,
    sweet the music.

> I hear the soughing   of the pine-trees
>   and pay no money;
> I am richer far   through Christ, my Lord,
>   than ever you were.
>
> Though you enjoy   all you consume
>   and wealth exceeding,
> I am grateful   for the riches
>   my dear Christ brings me.
>
> No hour of trouble   like you endure,
>   no din of combat:
> I thank the Prince   who so endows me
>   in my bothy.*

The hermit in his cell *(dísert,* from Latin *desertum)* kept away from the evil of his time without attempting to heal it. About the middle of the eighth century, however, and especially towards the end of it, efforts were made to reform monastic life, to restore it to its former severity and vigour. Some of the ancient monasteries, for example Lismore, not only reformed themselves but even played a leading part in the reform movement. In others, such as Armagh and Ros-Cré, one group of monks, who returned to the strict observance of old, separated from the rest; in Ros-Cré the stricter group retired to a lake-island, two miles away (Loch-Cré). Other places came into prominence only in the course of this movement; Finglas, for example, began to flourish under the reform bishops Caencomrac and Dublittir. The reform led also to new monastic foundations such as Tallaght, in the hills outside Dublin, during the third quarter of the century. Tallaght became the centre of the new movement, and its founder, Máel-Rúain (d. 792), as well as his disciple, Oengus, were prominent among the reformers. It was either in Tallaght or under the influence of its spirit that the most important literary documents of the reform movement came into existence: the Martyrology of Tallaght, the poetic calendar of feasts *(Félire)* of Oengus, a Penitential in Old Irish, and the list of *arras* (Latin: *arrea)* or "commutations" by which a severe penance of short duration could be substituted for a longer and milder one.

The reformed monks called themselves "Friends of God" *(Céli Dé,* Anglicized "Culdees"). They deliberately shifted the emphasis in monastic life from the intellectual and artistic interests of the older monasteries to the practice of ascetical piety. Among the Culdees we find for the first time a considerable amount of religious literature in the vernacular. Tallaght apparently housed many monks who were not priests and knew no Latin; some provisions of the Tallaght Penitential even suggest that not all of the brethren were able to read.

The spirit of the Culdees and the severity of the asceticism which they practised manifest themselves most impressively in the "Table of Commutations", from which I quote some extracts:

A commutation for rescuing a soul out of hell: three hundred and sixty-five Paters and three hundred and sixty-five genuflexions and three hundred and sixty-five blows of the scourge every day for a year, and a fast every month—this rescues a soul out of hell. For it is in proportion to the number of joints and sinews in the

* See note on p. 144

human body that this commutation to save a soul which has merited torments (while) in the body has been devised. . . .

Every penance is determined, both as to its severity and the length of time one is engaged in it, by the magnitude of the sin, the length of time it is persevered in, the motive for which it is committed, and the fervour with which it is eventually abandoned. For there are certain sins which are not entitled to any remission of the penitence due for them, however long be the period prescribed for them, unless God Himself shorten it by means of death or a message of sickness or the amount of (extra) mortification a person takes on himself. Such are, for example, kin-slayings, homicides, and secret murders; also brigandage, druidism and satirizing; further, adultery, incest, perjury, heresy, and violation of (the duties of one's ecclesiastical) grade. . . .

The sages enumerate four reasons why the commutations are practised: (1) for a speedy separation from the sin with which one has been united; (2) for fear of adding to the sin in the future; (3) for fear that one's life be cut short before the end of the penance decided by a soul-friend; (4) in order to (be free to) approach the Body and Blood of Christ by restricting (the period of) penance. . . .

As there is a difference between laymen and clerics and between nuns and laywomen, so too there is a difference between the (kind of) mortification and penance due from them, as well as between the commutations which may properly be performed by them.

First, commutations proper for former lay men and women: spending the night in water on nettles, or with a dead body—for there is hardly a single layman or laywoman who has not some share (of responsibility) for a manslaughter. On the other hand these are the commutations proper for clerics and nuns except such of them as have slain a man (who are required to perform the first kind)—unless, indeed (a commutation of the first kind) be performed for the purpose of increasing one's reward: spending the night in cold churches or remote cells while keeping vigils and praying without respite—as though one were at the very gates of hell—unless a little weariness chance to occur between two cycles of prayer, when one may sit.

These, now, are the commutations of a black fast (due) after grievous sin, as the saints have prescribed: a hundred blows with the scourge or (recitation of) the Three Fifties together with their hymns and canticles.

Another commutation (of the same): a hundred Paters (said while) in cross-vigil (that is, standing, with one's arms stretched out), and "Deus in adiutorium" as far as "festina" thrice at the conclusion of each Pater, and a genuflexion after each "Deus", and diligent meditation on God. For him who does this thrice it is a commutation of a three days' black fast.

Commutation of a three-days' fast for one who can read: (reciting) the Three Fifties standing and celebrating each canonical hour, twelve genuflexions with arms outstretched towards God at each canonical hour and diligent meditation upon heaven.

Commutation of a black fast (due) for grievous sin for one who cannot read: three hundred genuflexions and three hundred properly administered blows with a scourge, at the end of each hundred a cross-vigil until the arms are weary. "I beseech pardon of God", "May I receive mercy", "I believe in the Trinity"—that is what one sings without ceasing until the commutation is completed; further, frequent striking of the breast and perfect contrition to God. To do this thrice is a commutation of a three days' fast. . . .

Another commutation of seven years' strict penance: seven months (passed) in confinement on bread and water (prostrate) on the soil or on the floor from one period of nones to another, together with fervent prayer and celebration of each canonical. . . .

If there be danger of death, the following is a commutation of a year (of penance) when accompanied by intense contrition: to chant 365 Paters standing with both arms extended towards heaven and without the elbows ever touching the sides, together with fervent concentration on God. And the words are not spoken aloud. And to recite the "Beati" in a stooping position with thy two arms laid flat by thy sides. Or the whole body is stretched out along the ground face downwards and both arms laid flat by the sides. Patrick has recommended this (type of) vigil and Columcille and Maedóc of Ferns and Molacca Menn and Brénainn moccu Altae....

Examples of such extreme asceticism were told of some of the ancient saints of Ireland; others would have been attributed to them under the influence of this new ascetical movement. The habit, for example, of reciting the entire Psalter while standing in icy water is reported in the Lives of so many Irish saints that we must assume it to have been a custom actually practised. Later centuries were rather shocked at such excessive physical mortification; one of the copyists of the Old Irish Penitential comments on a severe penance which it prescribes: "Hard art thou, o Penitential!"

The Céli Dé might have brought about a thorough-going reform of monasticism in the entire country but for the coming of the "Norsemen", who from 795 onwards ravaged more and more often the shores and estuaries of Ireland, and about 840 even settled down in Dublin. Churches and monasteries were plundered and burnt to the ground. Monks and scholars fled in large numbers to the Frankish kingdom, which was then beginning to thrive. The insecurity of life had a demoralizing effect on those who stayed at home, and the monastic reform movement died out before it had come to full maturity. Not until the beginning of the eleventh century, when Brian Ború defeated the Danes at Clontarf, was the reform of the Irish Church to gather new momentum. This reform, however, which was implemented by the Synod of Kells (1152), was linked up closely with Canterbury and Rome and with the introduction of the new continental orders, and primarily that of the Cistercians. The protagonist of that reform, Bishop Malachy of Armagh, was indeed a good friend of St. Bernard of Clairvaux. From then on Ireland became fully integrated into Western Christendom, and the Irish Church no longer differed much from the Church in other countries.

The ideals of early Irish monasticism were preserved intact by the numerous monks who during the seventh and eighth centuries left Ireland for the Continent. This great expansion of Irish Christianity, which began with Columba and Columbanus in the later years of the sixth century, will be described in the next chapter. The present one might well be concluded with a poem which a monk of Bangor wrote in praise of his monastery:

Good rule of Bangor,
straight and divine,
holy, exact and constant,
exalted, just and admirable.

Blessed family of Bangor,
founded on unerring faith,
adorned with salvation's hope,
perfect in charity.

Ship never distressed
though beaten by the waves;
fully prepared for nuptials,
spouse for the sovereign Lord.

House full of delicious things
and built upon a rock;
and no less the true vine
brought out of Egypt's land.

Surely an enduring city,
strong and unified,
worthy and glorious,
set upon a hill.

Ark shaded by Cherubim,
all overlaid with gold,
filled with the sacred things
and borne by four men.

A very queen for Christ
clad in the light of sun,
innocent yet wise,
from every side invulnerable.

A truly regal hall
with many jewels adorned,
of Christ's flock too the fold,
and kept by the great God.

A virgin fruitful she
and mother undefiled,
joyful and tremulous,
submissive to God's word.

For whom with the perfect
a happy life is destined,
prepared by God the Father,
to last to eternity.

*Good rule of Bangor.**

Initial from the Book of Kells.

* The initial line of the poem is repeated at the end in order to indicate that its first stanza is to be recited once more. This antiphonal structure is characteristic of all Irish poetry, whether it is in Latin or in Irish.

PIONEERS OF IRISH CHRISTIANITY ABROAD
COLUMBA AND COLUMBANUS

 EFORE the end of the sixth century Irish monasticism had begun to expand beyond the shores of Ireland. It was only one step from settling on a stony island like Áramór or Skellig (where the homeland was still in sight) to real emigration. The goal of this emigration was for some Scotland and the islands off her western and northern coast, and for some the Continent of Europe. The legend of St. Brendan in all probability started from the saint's intention to retire to a remote island in the ocean, and the later *Voyage of Brendan* has as its historical nucleus the emigration of Irish monks to the Hebrides, the Faroe Islands, and Iceland during the seventh and eighth centuries. It is less certain that there were Irish monks in France before Columbanus, and the nationality of allegedly Irish saints in Italy during the same period—Ursus of Aosta, Frediano of Lucca, Cathaldus of Taranto—is questionable.

The emigration of St. Columba or Columcille to Iona (Hy) in 563 or 565, and that of St. Columbanus and his companions to the Frankish kingdom in about 590, and thence to Lombard-ruled Italy, are known on excellent historical authority. The work of these two monks and their successors shaped decisively the religious and cultural life of England and of Western and Central Europe for several centuries.

Both have the same (monastic) name, which means "Dove" (Columcille: "Dove of the Church"). They are comparable also in many other respects. Both have the background of Irish nobility: Columbanus came from a noble family in Leinster, Columba from the Cenél Conaill, a branch of the royal family of the Uí Néill. Both were scholars and poets. Both left their country in order to "live in exile for Christ". Both became missionaries in their chosen places of exile and made them centres for the expansion of Christianity: from Iona the Gospel was preached to the Scots and the Northumbrians, and Columbanus's disciple Gallus converted the Alemanni on the Upper Rhine.

Fortunately for the historian, both saints found biographers who rise considerably above the level of the average hagiographer. Adamnán's *Life of St. Columba* has already been mentioned. The *Vita* of St. Columbanus is even nearer the saint's time than is Adamnán's work to the lifetime of Columcille. The former was written in about 640 by a certain Jonas, who had become a monk at Bobbio shortly after Columbanus's death, and had been secretary to the first two successors of the founder. Jonas also knew personally St. Gall and other disciples of Columbanus. This is not to say that either Adamnán or Jonas has given us a biography in the modern sense; we must always make allowance for the conventions of the hagiographical genre and for the authors' preoccupation with asceticism and with the miraculous. However, even though neither tells us as much about the external life of his hero as we would like to know, both are perfectly trustworthy with regard to the details which they chose to record.

When Columcille left Ireland, he parted from his country but not from his people. Only the island of Mull separated Iona from the coast of Scotland, where the Northern Irish Dáil Riada had founded a colony. Their new ruler, Aidán mac Gabráin, was crowned by Columba, a prerogative which he passed on to his successors; the Abbot of Iona was, so to say, the Primate of Dáil Riada.

I have mentioned already the legend that Columcille went into lifelong exile as a penance for having caused the battle of Cúl Dreimne. This legend is the basis of a number of poems—the earliest date from the ninth century—which are put in Columba's mouth (a poetical fiction, not a forgery), for example:

Grey eye there is
that backward turns and gazes;
never shall it see again
Ireland's women, Ireland's men.

His thoughts, however, turn again and again to his beloved Ireland:

This were pleasant, O Son of God,
*   with wondrous coursing*
to fare across the swelling torrent
*   back to Ireland.*

To Eolarg's plain, past Benevanagh,
*   across Loch Feval,*
and there to hear the swans in chorus
*   chanting music.*

And when my boat, the Derag Drúchtach,
*   at last made harbour*
in Port na Ferag the joyful seagulls
*   would sound a welcome.*

I ever long for the land of Ireland
*   where I had power,*
an exile now in midst of strangers,
*   sad and tearful.*

Woe that journey forced upon me,
*   O King of Secrets;*
would to God I'd never gone there,
*   to Cooldrevne.*

Well it is for son of Dímma
*   in his cloister,*
and happy I but were I hearing
*   with him in Durrow*

The wind that ever plays us music
*   in the elm-trees,*

Ornaments from the Book of Kells.

66

and sudden cry of startled blackbird,
    wing a-beating.

And listen early in Ros Grencha
    to stags a-belling,
and when cuckoo, at brink of summer,
    joins in chorus.

I have loved the land of Ireland
    —I cry for parting;
to sleep at Comgall's, visit Canice,
    this were pleasant.

Initial from the Book of Kells.

In actual fact Columba did not cut his links with the country of his birth for good. The numerous churches and monasteries which he had founded in Ireland before he went into exile were governed from Iona. Messengers of the founder would frequently go to and fro, and occasionally the saint had to go in person. As a member of the highest aristocracy, Columba continued to be involved in the political and cultural life of Ireland. Adamnán and other writers testify to his presence at the assembly of Druim-Cetta (574 or 587), where he acted as mediator between the Irish at home and the colonists across the sea, and where, it is said, he saved the order of poets *(filid)* from suppression. More important for the future was the fact that he converted the Picts, whose territory lay to the north of Dáil Riada, and that by doing so he laid the foundations of a Christian Church in Scotland—the first great achievement of Irish monasticism away from home. Down to the eighth century Columba and his successors held a place of honour within the Irish Church that was challenged by none.

Columba's memory was honoured equally in the country of his exile. In Bede's Ecclesiastical History we read the following appreciation:

For in the 565th year of the Lord's incarnation (at which time Justin the younger, succeeding Justinian, received the governance of the Roman empire), there came to Britain from Ireland a priest and abbot notable by his dress and life of a monk, called Columba, to preach the word of God to the provinces of the northern Picts, that is to say, to those that by high and hideous ridges of hills were disseevered from the southern regions inhabited by Picts....

Now Columba came to Britain when the most puissant king Bruide, Maelchon's son, reigned over the Picts in the ninth year of his reign, and did by word and example convert the nation to the faith of Christ: in consideration whereof too the aforesaid isle (Iona) was given to him in possession to make a monastery. For the isle is not great either, but as though it were of five households by estimation of the English; and his successors keep it until this day, and there he himself lieth buried, dying at the age of seventy-seven years, about thirty-two years after that he came to Britain to preach. But before that he travelled to Britain, he had made a famous monastery in Ireland, which for the great store of oaks is in the Scottish tongue called Dearmach (Durrow), that is to say, the field of oaks. Of both the which monasteries very many more religious houses were afterwards built in addition by his scholars both in Britain and in Ireland; of all the which, the same monastery that is in the isle wherein his body lieth is the head house.

Moreover, the same isle is always wont to have an abbot that is a priest to be the ruler, to whose law both the whole district and also the bishops themselves ought, after an unaccustomed order, to be subject, according to the example of the first teacher who was no bishop, but a priest and monk: of whose life and sayings the report is that some things remain written by his scholars.

We would give much for a fuller knowledge of the life of this powerful and impressive personality. Bede's homage, for all its interesting detail, does not satisfy us. Adamnán in his *Life of St. Columba* conforms with hagiographical tradition to such an extent that he relates on the whole nothing but isolated stories of miracles in which the saint's power is manifested in one way or another. He rises to the stature of a biographer only in the long final chapter in which he gives an account, vivid as well as moving, of Columba's last days:

CONCERNING THE PASSING TO THE LORD OF OUR HOLY PATRON COLUMBA

When the end was drawing near of the four years above-mentioned, after the completion of which the foreteller of truth had long ago foreknown that his present life would come to a close, one day, in the month of May, as we have written in the preceding second book, the saint went, drawn in a wagon (being an old man, weary with age), to visit the labouring brothers, at work in the western part of the island of Io; and on that day he began to speak to them in this manner, saying: "At the Easter festival recently held, in the month of April, I desired with desire to depart to Christ the Lord, as had indeed been granted by him to me, if I had so chosen; but I chose rather to put off a little longer the day of my departure from the world, so that the festival of joy should not be turned for you into sorrow." Meanwhile the monks of his congregation that heard him speak these sad things became very sorrowful; and he began to cheer them, as well as he could, with comforting words. After which, still sitting in the wagon, he turned his face to the east, and blessed the island, with the islanders its inhabitants. And from then to the present day, as has been written in the above-mentioned book, the poison of three-forked tongues of vipers has not been able to do any injury to either man or beast. After the words of this blessing, the saint was carried back to his monastery.

Then after a few days had passed, while the rites of the Mass were being celebrated on a Lord's-day according to the custom, the venerable man lifted up his eyes, and suddenly his face was seen to flush with a ruddy glow; for, as it is written, "The countenance glows when the heart is glad"; and in fact at the same moment he alone saw an angel of the Lord hovering above, within the walls of the oratory itself; and because the calm and lovely sight of holy angels fills the hearts of the elect with joy and exultation, this was the cause of the sudden gladness that filled the blessed man. When those that were present there asked about this, the cause of the gladness inspired in him, the saint, gazing upward, gave them this reply: "Wonderful and incomparable is the fineness of angelic nature! See, an angel of the Lord, sent to recover a deposit dear to God, looking down upon us within the church and blessing us, has returned through the roof-courses of the church, leaving no trace of that departure." This the saint said, but yet none of those standing by could know of what kind that deposit was, to recover which the angel had been sent. Our patron, however, described as a "deposit" his own holy soul, entrusted to him by God, which, as will be related below, departed to the Lord after an interval of six consecutive days, on the Lord's-night following.

In the end of the same week, that is, on the Sabbath day, the venerable man himself, and his devoted attendant Diormit, went to bless the nearest barn. After entering it, and blessing it and two heaps of grain that were there in store, the saint spoke thus, and rendering thanks said: "I greatly congratulate my family of monks, because in this year also, if I have to depart from you to any place, you will have enough (bread) for the year." When the attendant Diormit heard this, he began to be sorrowful, and to speak in this manner: "This year, father, you very often sadden us, because you frequently speak of your passing." The saint gave him this answer: "I have a few secret words concerning my departure that I shall be able to communicate somewhat more plainly to you, if you will faithfully promise me not to disclose them to any one before my death." After the attendant had completed that promise on bended knees, according to the saint's desire, the venerable man made a statement to this effect: "This day is called in the sacred books 'Sabbath', which is interpreted 'rest'. And truly this day

trib: pauci & ipsi eminus
ad stantes uidebant.
Conmittitur ergo ecclesiam
in gradient plebili ingemi
nat uoce ubi & sanctus sanc
dum allatus fratrum luctu
nis sanctus thebnas palpans san
ante altarium recubantem
inuenit quem paululus ...
& iuxta redeni sanctum in suo
gremio posuit caput. &
inter haec coetus monachorum
cum luminaribus: ad currens
patris uiro moribus conspe
planctus & ut ab aliquibus:
qui present erant in fine didi
cimus sanctus nec dum egredienti
te anima apertis rursum
oculis ad utrum que: latus cum
mira uultus hilaritate
& letitia circum respiciebat
rostro felices ob uisos in tuebitur
angelos. Conuersusque au
sanctam subleuat ad benedi
cendum sanctum monachorum cho
num dexteram manum. sed

& ipse uenerabilis pater
in quantum poterat simul
suam mouebat manum. ut
uidelicet quod uoce in ipse
su non ualebat anime
etiam motu manus sua
... uidebatur benedicere
& post sanctam benedictio
nem ... significatam
continuo spiritum ex alaui
quo tabernaculum corpo
ris egresso facies rubere
& minus in modum angelica
uisione exhilarata inter
... ut non quasi
mortui sed dormientis
uidebatur uiuentis. tota
interim psallebat m...
tis planctoribus: ecclesia. f
non ... uidetur
quod eadem hora beate
transitus anime cuidam
... sancto reuelata(m)
... illo nam que monas
...mio quod scotica no
minatur lingua cloni

is for me a Sabbath, because it is my last day of this present laborious life. In it after my toilsome labours I keep Sabbath; and at midnight of this following venerated Lord's-day, in the language of the Scriptures I shall go the way of the fathers. For now my Lord Jesus Christ deigns to invite me. To him I shall depart, I say, when he invites me, in the middle of this night. For so it has been revealed to me by the Lord himself." The attendant hearing these sad words began to weep bitterly, and the saint tried to comfort him, as well as he could.

After this, the saint left the barn, and returning towards the monastery sat down midway. In that place a cross that was later fixed in a mill-stone is seen, standing by the roadside, even today. And while the saint sat there, resting for a little while, being (as I have said above) weary with age, behold, a white horse came to him, the obedient servant who was accustomed to carry the milk-vessels between the cow-pasture and the monastery. It went to the saint, and strange to tell put its head in his bosom, inspired, as I believe, by God, before whom every living creature has understanding, with such perception of things as the Creator himself has decreed; and knowing that its master would presently depart from it, and that it should see him no more, it began to mourn, and like a human being to let tears fall freely on the lap of the saint, and foaming much, to weep aloud. When he saw this, the attendant began to drive away the weeping mourner; but the saint forbade him, saying: "Let him, let him that loves us, pour out the tears of most bitter grief here in my bosom. See, man though you are, and having a rational soul, you could by no means know anything of my departure except what I myself have even now disclosed to you. But to this brute and unreasoning animal the Creator has, in what way he would, revealed clearly that its master is going to depart from it." Thus speaking, he blessed his servant the horse, as it turned sadly away from him.

Going from there, and climbing a small hill which overlooked the monastery, he stood on its summit for a little while. And as he stood he raised both hands, and blessed his monastery, saying: "On this place, small and mean though it be, not only the kings of the Irish with their peoples, but also the rulers of barbarous and foreign nations, with their subjects, will bestow great and especial honour; also especial reverence will be bestowed by saints even of other churches."

After these words, he descended from that little hill, returned to the monastery, and sat in the hut, writing a psalter. And when he came to that verse of the thirty-third Psalm where it is written, "But they that seek the Lord shall not want for anything that is good", he said: "Here, at the end of the page, I must stop. Let Baithene write what follows." The last verse that he wrote aptly befits the holy predecessor, who will never lack eternal good things. And the verse that follows, "Come, my sons, hear me; I will teach you fear of the Lord", is fittingly adapted to the successor, the father of spiritual sons, a teacher, who, as his predecessor enjoined, succeeded him not in teaching only, but in writing also.

After he had written the former verse, at the end of the page, the saint entered the church for the vesper office of the Lord's-night. As soon as that was finished, he returned to his lodging, and reclined on his sleeping-place, where during the night he used to have, for bed, the bare rock; and for pillow, a stone, which even today stands beside his grave as a kind of epitaph. So while reclining there, he gave his last commands to the brothers, in the hearing of his attendant alone, and said: "I commend to you, my children, these latest words, that you shall have among yourselves mutual and unfeigned charity, with peace. If you follow this course after the example of the holy fathers, God, who gives strength to the good, will help you; and I, abiding with him, shall intercede for you. And not only will the necessaries of this life be sufficiently provided by him, but also the rewards of eternal good things will be bestowed, that are prepared for those who follow the divine commandments." We have carried down to this point, briefly told, the last words of the venerable patron, when he was, as it were, crossing over to the heavenly country from this weary pilgrimage.

After them the saint was silent for a little, as the happy latest hour drew near. Then, when the beaten bell resounded at midnight, he rose in haste and went to the church and, running, entered in advance of the others, alone; and bowing his knees in prayer he sank down beside the altar. In that moment Diormit, the attendant, following later, saw from a distance the whole church filled inside with angelic light about the saint. As Diormit approached the doorway, the light that he had seen quickly faded. A few more of the brothers also had seen it, when they too were a little way off. So Diormit entering the church cried in a tearful voice: "Where are you, where are you, father?" And groping in the darkness, since the lamps of the brothers had not yet been brought, he found the saint lying before the altar. Raising him a little, and sitting down beside him, he placed the holy head upon his lap. Meanwhile the company of monks ran up with lights; and when they saw that their father was dying they began to lament. And as we have learned from some men who were present there, the saint, whose soul had not yet departed, opened his eyes, and looked around on either side, with wonderful joy and gladness of countenance; for he was gazing upon the holy angels that had come to meet him. Then Diormit raised the holy right hand, to bless the saint's company of monks. And the venerable father himself at the same time moved his hand, as much as he was able, in order that he might be seen to bless the brothers even by the movement of his hand, a thing that in the departure of his soul he could not do by voice. And after the holy benediction thus ex-

pressed he presently breathed out his spirit. When that had left the tabernacle of the body, his face continued to be ruddy, and in a wonderful degree gladdened by the vision of angels, so much that it seemed like the face not of a dead man, but of a living sleeper. Meanwhile the whole church resounded with sorrowful lamentations.

This happened during the night of Saturday to Sunday, June 9, 597.

Columba left no didactic writings. He taught, as Bede tells us, by word and example. According to an old tradition, however, he was a *fili*, a member of the national guild of poets. Of the numerous Irish poems which are headed *Columcille cecinit* not a single one can be attributed to him with any degree of probability because they are all written in a language of much later date than the sixth century. Three Latin hymns that go under his name might, linguistically, well be of the sixth century, and for the most important of these, the hymn *Altus Prosator*, his authorship is quite arguable. This poem has twenty-three stanzas of six lines each. It is an abecedarian hymn, that is to say, the initials of its stanzas make up the alphabet. The theme of the hymn is the Christian's view of God and the world, from the divine nature before creation to the end of time. Its style is learned and often obscure; the poet's language abounds in rare words of the *Hisperica Famina* type. In contrast to this laboured idiom the effect is, on the whole, anything but poetical. Whatever poetry may be found in it derives mainly from the Bible, and especially from the Old Testament. Towards the end, however, the hymn does rise to the heights of poetry with a grandiose picture of the Last Things.

NORTHUMBRIA   Not so long after Columba's death Iona found a new mission field, Northumbria, the northernmost kingdom of the Anglo-Saxon heptarchy. In the course of dynastic wars between the rulers of its two provinces, Deira and Bernicia, the sons of Ethelfrid of Bernicia had fled to the Picts and the Irish of Dáil Riada and had been won for the Christian faith. However, when one of the brothers, Eanfrid, acceded to the throne of Bernicia in 633, he returned to paganism. Within a year he lost his throne to the Briton Ceadualla, who also defeated Osric of Deira and held both provinces under a rule of terror. In 635 Ceadualla was defeated by Eanfrid's brother Oswald and lost his life on the battlefield. For the continuation of the story let us turn to Bede:

The same Oswald therefore, as soon as he was come to the throne, being desirous that all the people whom he began to rule should be filled with the grace of the Christian faith, whereof he had now gotten very great proofs in vanquishing the barbarians, sent to the aldermen of the Scots, among whom he, living in banishment and the soldiers which were with him, had obtained the sacraments of baptism; making request unto them that they would send him a prelate, by whose teaching and ministry the English people which he ruled might both learn the gifts of our Lord's faith and receive the sacraments. And not long after he obtained what he sought: for he received Aidan as bishop, a man of marvellous meekness, godliness, and sobriety, and one that had the zeal of God, though not fully according to knowledge. For he was wont to keep Easter Sunday from the fourteenth day after the change of the moon until the twentieth according to the custom of his nation, whereof we have divers times made mention. For the north provinces of the Scots and all the nation of the Picts did at that time still solemnize Easter Sunday by that rule, thinking that in this keeping of Easter they had followed the advertisement written by the holy and praiseworthy father Anatolius.... Furthermore, the Scottish nations which dwelt in the southern parts of the isle of Ireland had long agone learned to keep Easter by the canonical approved custom, being advised thereto by the bishop of the apostolic see.

To bishop Aidan then, upon his coming, the king appointed his episcopal see in the island of Lindisfarne, where the bishop himself desired it to be. Which same place with flowing and ebbing of the tide is twice every day environed like an island with the surges, twice joined on the mainland, the shore being voided again of the sea waves. And so following humbly and readily in all things the advice of the bishop, the king set himself very diligently to build up and enlarge the Church of Christ in his realm. Wherein it often fell out that there was a gracious and pleasant sight seen, when the bishop, who was unskilful of the English tongue, was preaching the Gospel, and the king himself was interpreter of the heavenly word to his aldermen and thanes: for that by reason of his long banishment in Scotland he had by now come to understand the tongue quite well. Hereupon a greater number began as the days went on to come from the country of the Scots to Britain, and with great devotion to preach the word of faith to those provinces of the English over which king Oswald reigned, and as many of them as were endowed with the degree of priesthood to minister the grace of baptism to them that believed. Therefore churches were builded throughout the districts, the people flocked joyfully to hear the word, possessions were given by the king's bountifulness and pieces of land for the foundation of religious houses, and the little children of the English along with elder folks were instructed under Scottish teachers in the studies and observation of monastic rule.

For they were for the most part monks who had come to preach. Aidan the bishop was himself a monk, seeing that he had been sent from the island which is called Hy: the monastery of which island was no small time the head house of all the monasteries almost of the northern Scots and of all the Picts, and had the sovereignty in ruling of all their people. The which isle in very deed belongeth to the right of Britain, being severed from it with a narrowed sea, but by the free gift of the Picts, who inhabit those coasts of Britain, had been long ago handed over to the Scottish monks, in consideration that by the preaching of those monks they received the faith of Christ....

From this isle therefore, from the convent of these monks, Aidan was sent to instruct the province of the English in Christ, after he had received the order of bishop. At which time Seghine, abbot and priest, was head of the same monastery. Whereby among other lessons of living, Aidan left the clerks a most wholesome example of abstinence and continence; and this thing did chiefly commend his doctrine to all men, that the learning which he taught was correspondent to the life he led with his brethren. For he took no thought to gain anything of this world or to be enamoured of it. His joy was forthwith to give away to the poor that might meet him all that was granted him of kings or wealthy men of the world. He was wont to travel abroad through all places both in towns and country, not riding on horseback but walking on foot, except peradventure a greater need had forced him to ride: in order that, wherever he had espied any, whether rich or poor, as he walked, incontinent turning aside to these, either he allured them to the mystery of receiving the faith, if they were out of the faith, or strengthened them in their faith, if they were in it, and exhorted them no less in deeds than in words to almsgiving and the execution of good works.

Moreover, his life was so far removed from the slackness of our time, that all they which walked with him, were they professed into religion or were they laymen, must needs study; that is, bestow their time either in reading Scripture or in learning the Psalter. This was the daily exercise of him and of all who were with him, to what place so ever they came. And if by chance it happened (which yet happened seldom) that he were bidden to the king's banquet, he went in accompanied with one or two clerks; and after a short repast, he made speedily haste to read with his brethren or else went forth to pray. All men and women under religious rule, being at that time taught by his examples, took a custom all the year through, saving only the fifty days after Easter, to prolong their fasting the fourth and sixth days of the week until the ninth hour. If rich men had done anything amiss, he never for hope of honour or fear of displeasure spared to tell them of it; but with sharp rebuking amended them. Never was he wont to give any money to the great men of the world (making them only good cheer, if he had received any to hospitality), but rather such gifts as in money were liberally given him by rich men, he did either (as we have said) give them in a dole for the relief of the poor, or else he laid them out for the ransoming of those that had been wrongfully sold. Finally, many of such as he had ransomed by payment of money he made after his scholars, and by bringing them up in learning and virtue advanced them to the degree of priesthood.

When, in 651, Aidan died at Bebba, the Northumbrian capital, his body was taken to Lindisfarne and laid to rest in its cemetery; later, when a new basilica was built on the island, Aidan's body was transferred there and buried beside the altar. Aidan was followed by Finan, who also came from Iona. He built the new episcopal church; it was larger than the one which had been built by Aidan, but, like its predecessor, it was not made of stone but of oak-wood and had a thatched roof, in accordance with the Irish tradition. This church was subsequently dedicated to St. Peter by Archbishop Theodore, and was provided with a roof of lead by Bishop Eadberct. Finan and his successor Colmán completed the conversion of Northumbria and began to preach the Gospel in Mercia and Essex.

CONTRAST
BETWEEN THE
ANGLO-SAXON
AND IRISH
MISSIONS

The Anglo-Saxons in the south of the island had accepted Christianity much earlier. To them the faith had been brought by the monk Augustine, whom Pope Gregory the Great had sent to the Angles in 597. Augustine had begun his missionary work in Kent, where he had made Canterbury his ecclesiastical centre. The mission to Southern England had started directly from Rome and maintained close links with the See of Peter. Among these links there is an interesting detail of liturgical history. Augustine had brought to England the Roman Psalter, a pre-Vulgate translation from the Greek, which had survived in liturgical use at Rome for a long time when newer versions were used almost everywhere else. Interestingly enough, this Psalter came to be widely used in the early English Church, as is proved by the fact that most of the early manuscripts of this text, often provided with glosses or interlinear versions in Anglo-Saxon, were written in England.

When the Kentish mission advanced towards the north, the Roman missionaries encountered those from Iona. It did not take the Romans long to find out that the ecclesiastical customs of the Northumbrians and of their Irish masters differed considerably from their own, and they did not conceal their disapproval. The discrepancy was, of course, the inevitable result of the comparative isolation in which the Church had developed in the Celtic lands for nearly two centuries. In actual fact this was not so much a special development as a tenacious adherence to customs which once were fairly universal but which in the Church at large had become obsolete. Foremost among the dissensions of "Celts" and "Romans" were the form of the tonsure and the calculation of the Easter date. In the Celtic churches the cleric was tonsured "from ear to ear", which probably means that his hair was shorn in the front of the head only; the "Roman" tonsure left only a crown of hair around a shorn skull. This tonsure, the Roman missionaries maintained, had been introduced by St. Peter himself, whereas the "Celtic" tonsure was attributed to the apostle's great enemy, Simon Magus. In determining the date of Easter, the Church was faced with the problem of harmonizing the Jewish-Christian week of seven days with the cycle of lunar months and with the solar year. After a number of unsatisfactory solutions Victorius of Aquitaine in 457 worked out an Easter cycle of 532 years, which was given its definitive form by Dionysius Exiguus in the following century. The Irish, however, went on using an earlier cycle of only eighty-four years; they also differed in other details of the computus, e.g. in fixing the spring equinox on 25 March, and in celebrating Easter on the fourteenth day of the lunar month if this was a Sunday. In combination, these factors often caused a considerable difference between the Irish and Roman Easter dates in one and the same year. Bede gives a vivid picture of the conflict which ensued and of its eventual solution:

About this time there was raised a hot and constant disputation touching the observance of Easter, they who had come from Kent or from France affirming that the Scots kept the Easter Lord's day contrary to the accustomed manner of the universal Church. Among these there was a very earnest defender of the true Easter, one named Ronan, a Scot born but yet instructed fully in the rule of ecclesiastical truth in the parts of France and Italy; who coupling and disputing with Finan set many aright or inflamed them to a more careful inquiry of the truth: yet was he able in no way to correct Finan; nay, rather he exasperated him by his reproof, being a man of hasty

Bede's account of the Synod of Whitby (Streunaeshalch) in MS Lat. Q. v. I. 18 at Leningrad.

nature, and made him an open adversary of the truth. On the other hand James, once deacon (as we have shewn before) of the venerable archbishop Paulinus, with all whom he was able to instruct in the better way, observed the true and catholic Easter. Eanfled also, the queen, with her train observed after the same manner as she had seen it practised in Kent, having with her a priest of catholic observation out of Kent, by name Romanus: whereby, as is said, it happened sometimes in those days that in one year Easter was kept twice, and when the king was breaking his fast and solemnizing the Lord's Easter, then the queen and her company continued yet the fast and kept the day of palms. Yet this diversity of keeping Easter, as long as Aidan lived, was borne in patience of all men, who had come to know very well that, though he was not able to celebrate Easter contrary to the custom of those who had sent him, yet he set himself diligently to perform works of faith, mercy, and love according to the manner customable with all holy men: upon which consideration he was deservedly beloved of all men, even of those which varied from him about Easter: and was held in reverence not only of the common sort but also of the bishops themselves, Honorius of the men of Kent and Felix of the East English.

But after the death of Finan who came after Aidan, when Colmán succeeded to the bishopric, who also himself was sent from Scotland, there arose a sharper disputation about the observance of Easter as well as upon other rules of ecclesiastical life: by occasion whereof this inquiry rightly stirred the minds and hearts of many from fear, lest, having gained the name of Christians, they did run or had run in vain. The dispute reached too to the ears of the princes themselves, to wit of king Oswy and his son Alchfrid; of whom Oswy, being brought up and baptized of the Scots and right skilful also in their tongue, thought nothing better than the manner which they had taught. In his turn Alchfrid, having for his teacher in Christian instruction Wilfrid, a man of great learning (for he had both travelled to Rome on his first visit for the sake of ecclesiastical teaching and spent a long time at Lyons with Dalfinus, archbishop of France, of whom also he had taken the crown of ecclesiastical tonsure), knew that Wilfrid's teaching was rightly to be chosen rather than all the traditions of the Scots: wherefore also he had granted him a monastery of forty households in the place which is called Inhrypum; which place indeed a little before he had given to those which followed the Scots, to have in possession for a monastery. But because afterwards, when choice was offered to them, they preferred to depart and yield up the place rather than to change their accustomed manner, it was given by the prince to him whose life and teaching he held to be worthy thereof. About that time Agilbert, bishop of the West Saxons, of whom we have made mention before, a friend of king Alchfrid and of Wilfrid the abbot, had come to the province of Northumberland and was staying with them for a space; who also at the request of Alchfrid made Wilfrid a priest in his monastery aforesaid. Now Agilbert had with him a priest named Agatho. The question therefore concerning Easter and the tonsure and other ecclesiastical matters being there raised, it was agreed on both sides that in the monastery called Strenaeshalc (which is by interpretation Lighthouse Bay [Whitby], over which Hild, a woman vowed to God, was abbess), a synod should be kept for the deciding of this question. And thither came both the kings, namely, the father and the son; the bishops, Colmán with his clergy of Scotland, and Agilbert with Agatho and Wilfrid, priests. On the part of these last were James and Romanus: Hild the abbess with her company were of the Scottish part, whereon also was the venerable bishop Cedd long since ordained of the Scots, as we have shewn before, who in that assembly came forward also as a most watchful interpreter on both sides.

And first king Oswy said beforehand by way of preparation that it behoved those who were united in serving God to keep one rule of living and not to vary in celebrating the heavenly sacraments, who looked all for one kingdom in the heavens; but rather they should search out what was the truer tradition and this should be followed uniformly of everyone: and first he commanded his bishop Colmán to declare what his observation was, and from whence he drew the source thereof and whom he followed therein. Then Colmán saith: "The Easter which I am accustomed to observe I have received of my elders of whom I was sent hither bishop, and this all our fathers, men beloved of God, are known to have solemnized after the same manner. And this observation, that none may think it a light matter or to be rejected, is the selfsame which the blessed evangelist John, the disciple whom the Lord specially loved, kept, as we read, with all the churches over the which he was head." And when he spake these and such like words the king commanded also Agilbert to declare before them all the manner of his observation, whence it was that it had beginning and by what authority he followed it. Agilbert answered: "Let, I beseech you, my scholar, the priest Wilfrid, speak herein for me, for we both, along with all the other followers after the ecclesiastical tradition, who sit here, are of one mind; beside, he can better and more clearly express our opinion in the very tongue of the English, than I am able to do, using an interpreter." Then Wilfrid, the king commanding him to speak, thus began: "The Easter which we follow we have seen to be kept by all at Rome

INITIUM EU
ANGELI IHU
XPI FILII

custi

CE

scrift   runu   godes   rue

SICUT SCRIPTUM EST

INESAIA PROPHETA

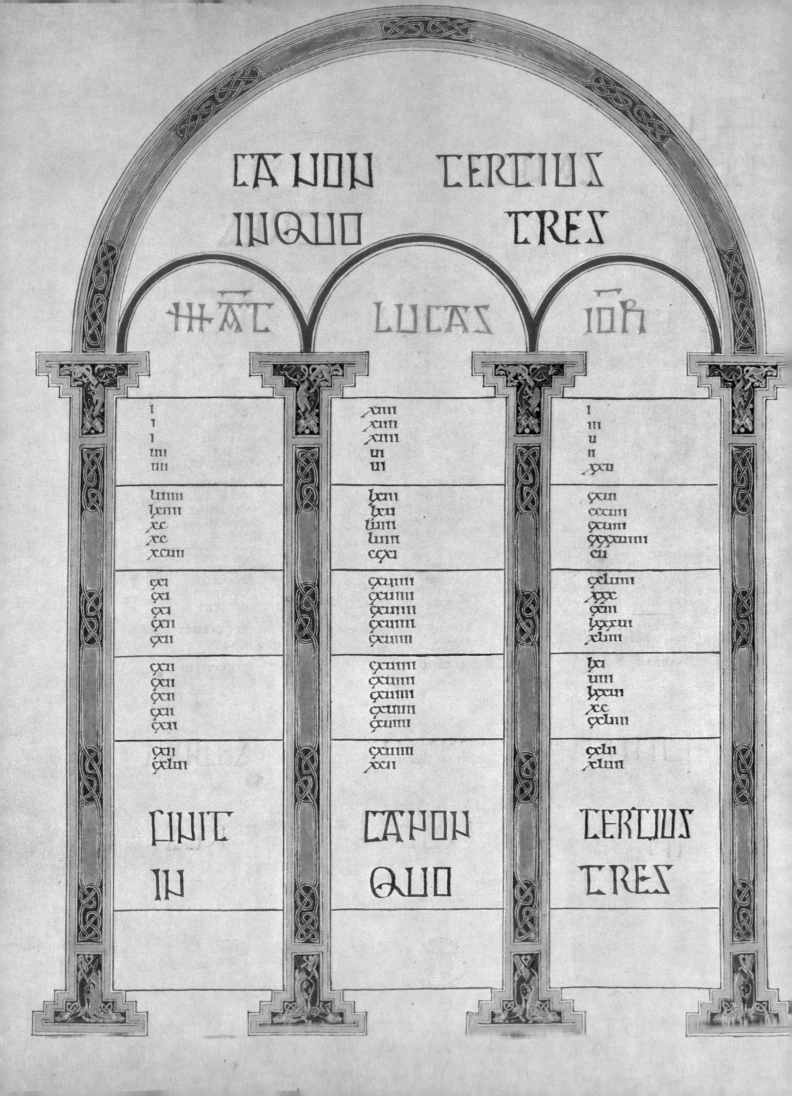

CANON TERCIUS
INQUO TRES

MAT   LUCAS   IŌH

MAT	LUCAS	IŌH
i	xiii	i
i	xiiii	iiii
iiii	iiii	iii
iiii	iii	ii
		xxii
lviiii	lxii	cxii
lxvii	lxi	ccciiii
xc	lviiii	cxiii
xc	lviiii	cccxviiii
xciiii	ccxi	cii
cxi	ccxiiii	ccliii
cxi	ccxiiii	xxx
cxi	ccxiii	cxii
cxi	ccxiiii	lxxvi
cxi	ccxiii	xliii
cxi	ccxiiii	lxi
cxi	ccxiii	viiii
cxi	ccxiiii	lxxii
cxi	ccxiii	xc
cxi	ccxiiii	ccliii
cxi	ccxiii	cclii
cxiiii	ccxiiii	cclii
ccliiii	xcii	xliiii

FINIT   CANON   TERCIUS
IN   QUO   TRES

where the blessed apostles Peter and Paul lived, taught, suffered and were buried: this manner we have noted to be practised of all in Italy, and in France, countries which we have passed through in pursuit of knowledge or desire to pray: this manner we have found to be performed in Africa, Asia, Egypt, Greece and all the world (wherever the Church of Christ hath been spread, throughout different nations and tongues), after one order of time and that without variableness: apart only from these men and them that are partakers of their obstinacy, the Picts I mean and the Britons, with whom, being natives of the two farthermost islands of the Ocean sea, and yet not the whole of them neither, these men with fond endeavour do contend against the whole world."

There follows a long, and rather technical, debate on the relative merits of the rival computations and their respective authority. The last speaker is Wilfrid. He does not deny the personal sanctity of the monks of Iona, but insists on the fact that though they err in good faith, they do err:

Wherefore also I deny not that they were servants of God and beloved of God, as the which loved God, though in rude simplicity, yet with a godly intention. Neither do I think that the manner of their observation of Easter is much prejudicial against them, as long as none had come to shew them the decrees of more perfect practice, the which they should follow: of whom I verily believe that had any catholic reckoner then come unto them, they would have followed his admonitions in the same manner in which they are shewn to have followed those commands of God which they knew and had learned. But as for thee and thy companions, if hearing the decrees of the apostolic see, nay, rather of the universal Church and these confirmed by Holy Writ, you scorn to follow them, you sin herein undoubtedly. For though thy fathers were holy men, is yet their fewness proceeding from one corner of the uttermost island of the earth to be put above the universal Church of Christ dispersed throughout the world? And if he your father Columba (yea, and our father if he was Christ's) was holy and mighty in works, can he by any means be chosen above the most blessed chief of the apostles, to whom our Lord said: "Thou art Peter, and upon this rock I will build my church, and the gates of hell shall not prevail against it, and I will give unto thee the keys of the kingdom of heaven" (Matth. 16.18–19)?

When Wilfrid thus concluded the king said: "Were these things, Colmán, indeed spoken to that Peter of our Lord?" And the bishop said: "They were indeed, my lord king." Whereat the king saith: "Can you bring forward any so special authority given your Columba?" Whereon the bishop said: "No." Again the king said: "Whether do ye both agree in this without any question, that these words were principally spoken unto Peter, and that unto him the keys of the kingdom of heaven were given of the Lord?" They answered: "Yea, certainly." Whereon the king thus concluded and said: "And I say unto you that I will not gainsay such a porter as this is; but as I know and have power, I covet in all points to obey his ordinances; lest it may be, when I come to the doors of the kingdom of heaven, I find none to open unto me, having his displeasure who is proved to hold the keys thereof."

When the king so spake, all that sat or stood by, the greater along with them of mean degree, gave their consent thereto; and abandoning their former imperfect usage hastened to change over to those things which they had learned to be better.

And the strife being thus ended and the assembly dissolved, Agilbert returned home. Colmán, seeing his doctrine contemned and sect reproved, taking those which would follow him, that is, which refused to accept the catholic Easter and the bearing of a shaven crown (for of this matter also there was no small disputation), returned unto Scotland, minding to deliberate there with his countrymen, what he ought to do concerning these matters. Cedd, forsaking the following of the Scots, returned to his see, inasmuch as he had embraced the observance of the catholic Easter. Now this controversy was moved in the 664th year of the Lord's incarnation, which was the twenty-second year of king Oswy; but in the thirtieth year after the Scots had been made bishops in the province of the English. For Aidan occupied his bishopric seventeen years, Finan ten and Colmán three.

As bishop of Northumbria, Colmán was replaced by Tuda, a pupil of the "Romanizing" Church of Southern England; as abbot of Lindisfarne, he was, at his own request, succeeded by Eata, former

Opposite:
A page with Eusebian Canons by the help of which parallel passages in the Gospels can be found, from the Lindisfarne Gospels.

abbot of Mailros (Melrose), one of the first twelve disciples of Aidan. Of Colmán himself Bede has something further to tell:

In the meantime Colmán, who was a Scottish bishop, left Britain and took with him all the Scots that he had gathered together in the isle of Lindisfarne: moreover, about thirty Englishmen, and all of either race were brought up in the exercises of monastical life and conversation. And leaving in his own church certain brethren, he came first to the isle of Hy, from whence he had been sent to preach the word to the English nation. Afterward he departed to a certain little isle which lieth on the west side, out of a good way from Ireland, and is called in the Scottish tongue Inisboufinde, that is to say, Whitecalf Isle. Into which he came and built a monastery, and placed the monks there, which he had brought with him and gathered of both nations. And, since they could not agree together (for that the Scots in summer-time, when harvest was to be got in, would leave the monastery and go wander abroad in places of their acquaintance, but of a truth, when winter approached, would come again and require to enjoy in common the things that the Englishmen had provided and laid up): Colmán, seeking remedy for this discord and viewing all places far and near, found a place in the island of Ireland meet for the building of a monastery, called in the Scottish tongue Mageo (Mayo); and of that ground he bought a small parcel to build a monastery thereon of the count that possessed the same: upon this condition withal, that the monks there abiding should make prayer to the Lord also for the lord of the soil who let them have that place. And the monastery being forthwith erected by the help also of the count and all such as dwelled thereby, Colmán placed the Englishmen there, the Scots being left in the foresaid island. The which monastery indeed unto this day is holden of English occupiers. For it is the selfsame which is now customably called Muigeo, being much enlarged of that it was at first, and (all things being long since brought to a better order) hath in it a notable company of monks gathered from the country of the English; who live therein after the example of the worthy old fathers, under a rule and canonical abbot, in great abstinence and singleness of heart by the labour of their own hands.

Iona resisted the Roman observance for a considerable time. Even Adamnán, who on one of his two visits to the court of King Aldfrid of Northumbria had been won over to the Roman discipline and who apparently, at an Irish synod held in 697, prevailed upon the churches of Northern Ireland to accept it, found it beyond his power to introduce the reform in his own monastery. Twelve years after Adamnán's death, a certain Ecgberct was more successful:

But when the most reverend and holy father and priest Egbert came to them from the English nation, living in exile for Christ a long time in Ireland, and being a man very well learned in the Scriptures and singular for the perfect life he led for many years, they were reformed by him and brought to keep Easter on the true and lawful day; nevertheless, they did not even before that time solemnize and keep it always upon the fourteenth day after the change of the moon, according to the Jews' custom (as some men supposed), but on the Sunday, though yet in another week than was convenient.

Dunchad, then abbot of Iona, in deference to Ecgberct, accepted the Roman rule, and in 716 the community of Iona for the first time celebrated Easter according to the Roman computus. It is uncertain, however, whether all the members of the community were on Dunchad's side. About this time a schism broke out among the Columban monasteries, and it is not unlikely that it was caused by dissension about the Easter date. In 717 Nectan, king of the Picts, who had accepted the Roman Easter in 710, expelled from his kingdom all those Columban monks who refused to conform.

Irish influence in Northumbria did not come to a sudden end at Whitby. Colmán emphasized his spiritual links with Lindisfarne by leaving there some part of the relics of Aidan when he himself had to go. His successor, Eata, came from Melrose, a daughter-house of Lindisfarne which had been founded during its "Celtic" period. Another monk of Melrose, St. Cuthbert, was bishop of Lindisfarne from 684 to 687. Both were staunch supporters of the Roman tradition, but both had also the background of Irish monasticism. In later legend Cuthbert was even made an Irishman. The strong imprint which the Irish left on the nascent Church of Northumbria is attested by Bede in his postscript to this important episode in the ecclesiastical history of England:

But how spareful persons he and his predecessors were and how greatly they abstained from all pleasures, even the place where they bare rule did witness, in the which at their departure very few houses were found beside the church; that is to say, those houses only without which the conversation of common life could nowise be maintained. They had no money, but cattle. For, if they took any money of rich men, by and by they gave it to poor people. For neither was it needful that either money should be gathered or houses provided for the entertainment of the powerful of this world, who never used to come to the church but only to pray and hear the word of God. The king himself, when occasion had required it, came accompanied with only five or six persons, and after prayer ended in the church departed. But if by chance it fortuned that they refreshed themselves there, they contented themselves only with the brethren's simple daily fare, looking for nothing farther. For then all the desire with those teachers was to serve God, not the world; their whole care was to comfort the heart, not the

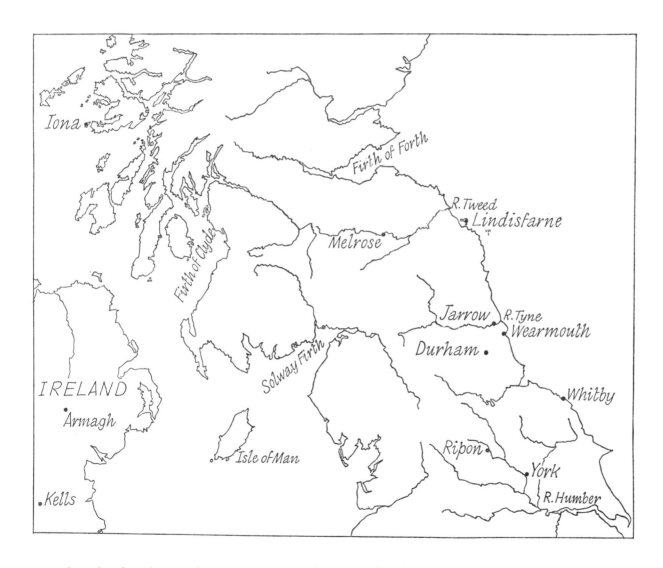

Map of Northumbria showing the more important Irish monastic foundations; in the north-west, the island of Iona.

paunch. Whereof it came to pass that in that time even the habit of religious men was had in great reverence; so that wherever any of the clergy or monks came, he was joyfully received of all men, like the servant of God: again, if any were found going on a journey, they ran unto him and making low obeisance rejoiced either to receive the sign from his hand or a blessing from his mouth; also they would diligently give ear to their words of exhortation. Moreover, too, upon the Sundays ordinarily the people flocked eagerly either to the church or to the monasteries, not for belly cheer but to hear the word of God: and if any of the priests came by chance abroad into the village, the inhabitants thereof would by and by gather together about him and set themselves to desire of him the word of life. For neither had either the priests themselves or the clergy other reason to come into the villages but only to preach, to baptize, to visit the sick, and (to speak all in one word) for the cure of souls: who were so far chastened from all the infection of covetousness, that none of them would take pieces of land and possessions toward the building of monasteries but through the constraint of the powerful of this world. Which custom in all points was maintained a long time hereafter in the churches of Northumbria. But thus much of these matters.

Another witness to the continued Irish influence in Northumbria is possibly the Book of Durrow. Most palaeographers and art historians agree that this manuscript, the first masterpiece of insular book-illumination that has survived, dates from the second half of the seventh century, and that it originated in a Columban community. But where was it written? In Ireland (Durrow), in Northumbria (Lindisfarne, Melrose), or in Iona? Durrow is suggested by the fact that our codex was there in the eleventh or twelfth century, when a Durrow deed was entered on one of its blank leaves, and that, in all probability, it was there already in 916, when King Flann had made for it a silver shrine. Suggestive of Iona is the relation, textually and artistically, between the Book of Durrow and the Book of Kells—if we accept the probable opinion that the latter was for the greater part written at Iona. Northumbrian origin was first suggested by the English theologian Burkitt, whose view was endorsed by so great an authority on the history of Latin script as E. A. Lowe. The basis of Burkitt's argument, namely the alleged "Northumbrian" Bible text of the Book of Durrow, has been shown to be of rather limited validity, but the palaeographical and artistic evidence is not so easily dismissed. The "Durrow" artist's contacts with Germanic art, which nobody denies, would have been made most naturally in Northumbria; the artistic and calligraphic style of this Gospel book has a great following in Northumbria and—apparently by way of Northumbria—in eighth-century Echternach. Even after the exodus of Colmán from Lindisfarne such a manuscript might have been produced there, and might later have found its way to Ireland. It is almost impossible to decide between these alternatives: the work of a Northumbrian scribe and illuminator cannot have differed greatly from that of his Irish master.

Some years after Whitby the English Church was temporarily subjected to a strong impulse from the Mediterranean world. In 669 Pope Vitalian appointed a Greek monk, Theodore, to the vacant see of Canterbury. The new Primate of England took with him Abbot Hadrian from Niridanum near Naples, a Hellenized African. Through Hadrian's teaching a new wave of Christian classicism pervaded England. Its results are manifest in the literary work of Hadrian's pupil, Aldhelm (d. 709), who had begun his studies under an Irish master named Máeldub or Máeldun. In Aldhelm the Hibernian and the Hellenic elements combined in a unique manner. In spite of his obscure and mannered Latinity, the Abbot of Malmesbury and Bishop of Sherborne was not only one of the most learned but also one of the most articulate writers of his time, and enjoyed the reputation of a great man of letters both at home and abroad.

The Northumbrian Benedict Biscop, who in 674 founded the monastery of Wearmouth and in 681 or 682 the twin monastery of Jarrow, also had links with Southern Italy. Being a man of keen and

The Eagle, symbol of the Evangelist John, in the Echternach Gospels, Bibliothèque Nationale, Paris.

far-reaching literary interests, he spared no effort in order to collect in his monasteries an excellent library. He made numerous journeys in search of manuscripts, and visited Italy several times. Benedict's efforts were continued by his successor, Ceolfrid. The latter died in 716 on a pilgrimage to Rome. He had with him a fine manuscript of the complete Vulgate Bible, which had been written in one of his monasteries and was to be presented to the Pope. The manuscript never reached its destination; it was later found at Monte Amiato, whence it passed into the Laurentian Library at Florence. This "Codex Amiatinus" is a most impressive witness to the new spirit of learning and of artistic creation in Northumbria. The text, especially in the Gospels – is purest Vulgate; it is derived from a South Italian exemplar, and is apparently modelled on a Bible codex of the great scholar Cassiodorus. The script is a calligraphic uncial, of the best Italian type, with rustic capitals as a display script. The illumination (most strikingly in the "portrait" of Ezra) continues the realistic, quasi-three-dimensional painting of late antiquity.

In about 680 Bede, then a boy of seven years, entered the monastic school at Wearmouth. There, and in the neighbouring Jarrow, he spent his days in the seclusion of the cloister, as a monk, priest, and scholar, until his death in 735. He is the most widely-read, the most comprehensive, and perhaps the most human author of the "Dark Ages". As an interpreter of the Bible and an encyclopedic writer, as a composer of hymns and of homilies, as a scientist and computist, but above all as the historian of the English Church, he holds a place of honour in the Latin literature of the early Middle Ages. For centuries his works have been an inspiration and a stimulus to readers throughout Western Christendom. Bede was no longer under the direct influence of the Irish mission, and his attitude to the Irish is rather reserved. He could not help being impressed by the religious zeal of the Irish monks, but on the whole he speaks of them in a slightly condescending manner. Whatever good he has to say about them is therefore doubly valuable as evidence.

Lindisfarne was not entirely by-passed by the Italian wave, but its Celtic tradition was strong enough to hold its own and to assimilate the Mediterranean influences rather than to succumb to them. The Lindisfarne Gospels, written—as the tenth-century glossator Aldred tells us—by Bishop Eadfrith (698–721) and bound by Bishop Eathelwald (724–740), present the same pure Vulgate text as does Codex Amiatinus. Pictorial illustration, in particular the "portraits" of the evangelists, derives unmistakably from the art of the South. Script and ornament, however, are entirely in the Celtic tradition. Nevertheless the "Lindisfarne" style, when compared with that of the Books of Durrow and Kells, strikes us as specifically "English": the regularity of its design, the neat arrangement of the text, the economy of planning, but also a certain sobriety, which at times is almost pedestrian, separate this manuscript, in spite of its Celtic heritage, from genuine Celtic work.

The Church of Northumbria followed the Irish Church in her missionary spirit. The starting-point, here as there, was the idea of an "exile for Christ". Ecgberct had left his native Anglia for Ireland, where he played an important part among the pro-Roman ecclesiastics of the South. Although he himself did not go *ad partes infidelium*, he was instrumental in starting a mission which turned out to be as important in the history of culture as it was in the history of religion. He exhorted a Northumbrian, Willibrord, who had been reared in the monastery of Ripon and then in 678 had gone to Southern Ireland for further study, to preach the Gospel among the pagan Frisians. About the time when Willibrord came to Ireland, Wilfrid (whom we have known as spokesman for Rome at Whitby) had already begun this work during a temporary stay in Frisia. Now (690) Willibrord revived the efforts of Wilfrid with new vigour. He founded the episcopal see of Utrecht and the monastery of Echternach (in present-day Luxemburg); the latter soon became a centre of Anglo-Saxon and Irish culture. The Calendar and Martyrology of Willibrord and the Echternach Gospels (now in the Bibliothèque Nationale, Paris) are lasting monuments to Willibrord's mission and its insular background. The mission to the Frisians attracted also the West Saxon Wynfrith (Boniface). His life-work began among the Frisians, in 716; he returned to them after completing his great task, the ecclesiastical organization of Germany, and was martyred there in 754.

The Anglo-Saxon mission to Europe contained, as we have seen, a conspicuous Irish strain. At home also the links with the Irish were never completely severed. This is especially true of Northumbria. Relations with Southern Ireland, where conformity with Rome had gained the upper hand as early as 630, had always been friendly, and those with the North must have been resumed when, in the late seventh century, the Roman customs were accepted and thus the cause of the temporary estrangement was resolved. There were Irish teachers and, apparently, Irish students at York as late as Alcuin's student years. These Irish associations were not forgotten when Alcuin became the head of the Palace School of Charlemagne.

The Angles and Saxons owed to the Irish not only the idea of spiritual exile in the form of foreign missions but also the choice of the Continent as their mission field. Almost exactly a hundred years before Willibrord set out for the conversion of the Frisians, Columbanus with twelve companions had landed on the coast of France. Their history is in many respects a repetition, though in rather different surroundings, of the history of Columba and his followers. Columbanus, however, was a very different character: fiery, rash, polemical, uncompromising, but none the less capable of deep and even gentle feeling. Wherever he went, he left traces as strong and as lasting as those of his namesake in the North.

Columbanus was born in Leinster in about 543. He probably came from a noble family. This is not stated expressly by his biographer, but it may be concluded from the fact that at an early age, long before his vocation to the monastic life, he was given a higher education. As a young man he strongly felt the stimulus of sensual desire; but a conversation which he once had with a woman hermit made him realize his vocation. Over the body of his mother, who threw herself across the threshold of the house, he made his way to the monastery. His first teacher was Sinell, a disciple of Finnian. Later Columbanus placed himself under the severe discipline of St. Comgall at Bangor, where he spent many years. He was already in the zenith of his life and had gained a great reputation as a teacher when he began to "desire exile". Although Comgall was sorry to see Columbanus go, he gave his consent. Columbanus left Bangor with twelve companions. After a short stay in Britain, they crossed to France. The most probable date of Columbanus's arrival in the Merovingian kingdom is 591.

The Franks were for the greater part nominal Christians, but the political and moral conditions of their country belied the religion which they professed. Repeated partitions of the kingdom among the members of the royal house and the dynastic quarrels which were the inevitable result, a decadent nobility, and a worldly clergy would arouse the religious zeal of such a man as Columbanus. He first went to the court of Childebert II of Burgundy and Austrasia. Impressed by Columbanus's preaching, the king asked the stranger to settle down in his country. Columbanus retired to the solitary mountain district of the Vosges. There, among the ruins of a Roman fort, he founded his first monastery at Anagrates (Annegray). Soon he began to attract followers. The number of those who gathered around him grew so fast that before long Annegray was too small for them. A bigger monastery was founded some miles away on the site of the ancient Luxovium (Luxeuil). His monks lived according to the Irish tradition. The monastery housed also lay penitents who preferred the Irish penitential practice to the customary public penance, and the sons of nobles who had been sent there for their education. For his monks, as we have seen, Columbanus wrote a rule, which is probably the earliest Irish monastic rule that was laid down in writing. His Penitential is concerned with both monks and lay people.

The clergy of Gaul did not look favourably at the Columban monasteries. To a continental ecclesiastic they must indeed have given offence in many respects. Unlike the Frankish monasteries, the foundations of Columbanus did not place themselves under the jurisdiction of the bishop in whose diocese they had been established. There was even a bishop among Columbanus's own monks, who, according to Irish monastic custom, conferred holy orders and exercised many other episcopal functions. The popularity of the Irishman's pastoral work and, in particular, of the Irish penitential practice, which to the Frankish prelates must have appeared highly irregular, was another cause for complaint. Finally, the Irish celebrated Easter according to a different computus from that of the Franks.

During the lifetime of Childebert nobody dared to proceed openly against the king's protégé; and when, some years after Childebert's death, it was decided to take action, the more fundamental points of difference were deliberately avoided and the attack was directed solely against Columbanus's allegedly heretical Easter date. Columbanus anticipated the attack and prevented a formal accusation by an appeal to Pope Gregory the Great (600). This letter of appeal is characteristic not only of Columbanus but of the attitude of the Irish Church as a whole. There is no trace of antagonism to Rome, as has sometimes been asserted. On the contrary, in this as in later letters, and especially in the fifth letter, which is addressed to Pope Boniface, Columbanus never tires of expressing most eloquently, but at the same time with perfect sincerity, his loyalty to the heir of Peter. Columbanus is firm, however, in his contention that his own people, contrary to other nations, have faithfully preserved the ancient Catholic tradition, pure and unadulterated. The Pope did not reply in person, but placed Columbanus under the protection of Abbot Conon of Lérins. Some years later (603) Columbanus was again attacked; this time the leading spirit was the newly appointed bishop of Lyons, Arigius. Columbanus was ordered to defend himself before a synod that was being held at Châlon. Anxious to avoid a personal appearance, Columbanus addressed to the synod an open letter. So far from arguing his case, he merely asked that he and his monks should be allowed to live in peace according to the monastic traditions of their own native country:

One thing therefore I request of your holiness, that with peace and charity you bear my ignorance and, as some say, my proud impudence in writing, which has been extorted by necessity, not pride, as my very baseness proves; and since I am not the author of this difference, and it is for the sake of Christ the Saviour, our common Lord and God, that I have entered these lands a pilgrim, I beseech you by our common Lord, and entreat you by Him who is to judge the quick and the dead, if you deserve His recognition, who shall say to many, Amen I say to you that I never knew you, that I may be allowed with your peace and charity to enjoy the silence of these woods and to live beside the bones of our seventeen dead brethren, even as up till now we have been allowed to live twelve years among you, so that, as up till now we have done, we may pray for you as we ought. Let Gaul, I beg, contain us side by side, whom the kingdom of heaven shall contain, if our deserts are good; for we have one kingdom promised and one hope of our calling in Christ, with whom we shall together reign, if indeed we first suffer here with Him, that also together with Him we may be glorified. I know that to many this verbosity of mine will seem excessive; but I judged it better that you too should know what we here discuss and ponder amongst ourselves. For these are our rules, the commands of the Lord and the apostles, in these our confidence is placed; these are our weapons, shield and sword, these are our defence; these brought us from our native land; these here too we seek to maintain, though laxly; in these we pray and hope to continue up till death, as we have seen our predecessors do. But do you, holy fathers, look what you do to your poor veterans and aged pilgrims; as I judge, it will be better for you to comfort them than to confound.

Childebert's son, Theuderic II, who had acceded to the throne of Burgundy after his father's death, showed great respect for Columbanus until the saint refused to bless Theuderic's illegitimate sons and thus to declare them, as it were, worthy of the throne. By this refusal Columbanus not only lost the favour of the king but also earned the hatred of the queen-grandmother, the still powerful Brunhild. Enraged by Columbanus's uncompromising moral attitude and undiplomatic insistence on his refusal, the king expelled the Irish abbot from his territory. From Besançon, where he was kept in temporary confinement, Columbanus succeeded in escaping and returning to Luxeuil. However, when the king was informed of this event, he ordered Columbanus to be forcibly sent back to Ireland. Partly by land and partly on the River Loire Columbanus and some of his brethren who had come with him from Ireland were brought by a military escort to Nantes, where a ship was to take them back to their country. On the point of departure Columbanus wrote to the monks who had stayed behind at Luxeuil the following letter of farewell:

To his most sweet Sons and dearest disciples, to the careful Brethren, to all his Monks together Columba the Sinner sends Greeting in Christ.

Peace be to you, as was the Lord's wish when He spoke to His disciples, and salvation and eternal charity. With Him may the Trinity grant you these three gifts, and preserve them amongst you with my prayer. The greatness of my zeal for your salvation is known to Him alone who gave it, and my longing for the advance of your instruction; but since, in accordance with the Lord's teaching, Tribulation and persecution have arisen for the word's sake, no other advice is now fitting for you, save that you beware lest you be that stony ground, which through the poorness of its soil cannot nourish the seed which it receives.... We ourselves know that we

86

donauit corpus ihū ioseph
Joseph autem mercatus est sin
donem et deponens eum in
uoluit in sindonem et possuit eū
in monumento quod excisum erat
de petra et aduoluit lapidem ad
ostium monumentī et abiit
Maria autem magdalenae
et maria ioseph aspicie
bant ubi poneretur
VI Et cum transisset sabbatū
maria magdalenae et ma
ria iacobi et salome emerunt a
romata ut uenientes ungerent eū
Et ualde mane una sabba
torum ueniunt ad monu
mentum orto iam sole et dicebā
nt

have received the Lord's word with gladness and enthusiasm; let us beware now lest we be short-lived. Patience is needful for us, that the proof of our faith, as it is written (1 Peter 1.7), may be more precious than gold.... And do not hope that it is men alone who persecute you; there are devils in those who envy your possessions.... Look to it that you be one heart and one mind, so that you may receive as a present reward whatever saving grace you seek from the Father of our Lord Jesus Christ.... Otherwise if you do not possess one and the same purpose and aversion, it is better that you do not dwell together. Therefore I command you that all, whose heart's desire is to consent with me, and who know and love my sentiment, remain with my true follower Attala, and let it be for him to choose whether he remain there or wish to come after me; for he senses the peril of your souls; do you obey him. But if he wishes to come, let Waldelenus be prior, since he can quickly, with God's help, reach a settled understanding; but meanwhile beware, lest there be any with you who does not possess one purpose with you, whoever he may be; for we have been more harmed by those who were not of one mind amongst us.

You know, my dearest Attala, those who are a trouble to your feelings; depose them at once; yet depose them in peace and agreement with the rule; only honour Libranus and keep Waldelenus always; if he is there with the community, may God deal well with him, may he be humble, and give him my kiss, which then in his hurry he did not receive. But you have long known my purpose of instilling character; if you see some progress of souls with you, stay there; if you see dangers, come thence; but the dangers I mean are the dangers of disagreement; for I fear lest there too there be disagreement on account of Easter, lest perhaps, through the devil's tricks, they wish to divide you, if you do not keep peace with them; for now without me you seem to stand less firmly there. Therefore be wary, considering the time when they do not endure sound doctrine.... Thus do you be wiser; I do not wish you to undertake so great a burden, under which I have sweated; for you know already the smallness of my knowledge, like a drop, you have learnt that all advice is not suitable for all, since natures are diverse and men's types differ widely from each other.... Therefore do you be many-sided and adaptable for the direction of those who obey you with faith and love; but you must fear even their very love, because it will be dangerous to you. But there are troubles on every side, my dearest friend; there is danger if they hate, and danger if they love. You must know that both are real, either hatred or love from their side; peace perishes in hatred, and integrity in love. Hold yourself therefore to the impulse of the one desire which you know my heart desires.... Do you and all that are wholly mine observe these precepts; and for the sake of unity and humility, however many you be when Christ increases and multiplies your numbers, let all have regard to him who ministers to God beside the altar that was blessed by the holy bishop Aid....

I have written this because of the uncertain outcome of events.... I wanted to write you a tearful letter; but for the reason that I know your heart, I have simply mentioned necessary duties, hard of themselves and difficult, and have used another style, preferring to check than to encourage tears.... See, the tears well up, but it is better to check the fountain; for it is no part of a brave soldier to lament in battle....

Now as I write a messenger has reached me, saying that the ship is ready for me, in which I shall be borne unwilling to my country; but if I escape, there is no guard to prevent it; for they seem to desire this, that I should escape. If I am cast into the sea like Jonah, who himself is also called Columba in Hebrew, pray that someone may take the place of the whale to bring me back in safe concealment by a happy voyage, to restore your Jonah to the land he longs for.

But now my parchment letter is already forced to reach its end, though the greatness of my subject requires a more extensive treatment; love does not keep order, hence my missive is confused. I wished to say everything in short, but could not manage everything. What I wanted to write, I would not in view of the difference of your desires.... Do you examine your consciences, whether you are more pure and holy in my absence.... Otherwise if you see perfection farther removed from you than before, and fate has kept me away from you, and Attala is not strong enough to govern you; since your brethren are here in the neighbourhood of the Britons, unite yourselves all together in one party, whichever is the better, that you may the more readily strive against the vices and wiles

Opposite:
Detail from fol. 185 V
of the Book of Kells.

of the devil; and meanwhile let him be your leader whom you all have chosen, since, if I am free to do so, by God's will I shall make provision for you. But if the situation pleases you and God builds with you there, may you increase there with His blessing to thousands of thousands; pray for me, my beloved children, that I may live to God.

Subsequent events made Columbanus's words about his chances of escape appear almost prophetic. His ship had scarcely left the harbour when a storm forced it back, and the captain let Columbanus go. He betook himself to the court of King Clothar II of Neustria, where he was cordially received. Next Columbanus proceeded to Austrasia. At Metz, at the court of King Theudebert, he met again some of his monks from Luxeuil, who had been banned from Burgundy by Theuderic. Together they rowed up the Rhine, with the intention of settling down at Bregenz on Lake Constance. During that voyage on the Rhine Columbanus might have written the following boating song (if the poem is his, which is doubtful), a fine example of Christian spirit expressed in classical form:

See, cut in woods, through flood of twin-horned Rhine
passes the keel, and greased slips over seas—
> *Heave, men! And let resounding echo sound our "heave".*

The winds raise blasts, wild rain-storms wreak their spite
but ready strength of men subdues it all—
> *Heave, men! And let resounding echo sound our "heave".*

Clouds melt away and the harsh tempest stills,
effort tames all, great toil is conqueror—
> *Heave, men! And let resounding echo sound our "heave".*

Endure and keep yourselves for happy things;
ye suffered worse, and these too God shall end—
> *Heave, men! And let resounding echo sound our "heave".*

★　　★　　★

Thus acts the foul fiend: wearing out the heart
and with temptation shaking inmost parts—
> *Ye men, remember Christ with mind still sounding "heave".*

Stand firm in soul and spurn the foul fiend's tricks
and seek defence in virtue's armoury—
> *Ye men, remember Christ with mind still sounding "heave".*

Firm faith will conquer all and blessed zeal
and the old fiend yielding breaks at last his darts—
> *Ye men, remember Christ with mind still sounding "heave".*

Supreme, of virtues King, and fount of things,
He promises in strife, gives prize in victory—
> *Ye men, remember Christ with mind still sounding "heave".*

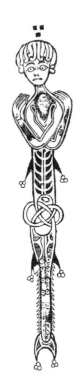

Mermaid from the Book of Kells.

The district around Lake Constance was still almost entirely pagan. Here, as during a short stay at Tuggen on Lake Zürich, the Irish met with fierce opposition. The victory of Theuderic over Theudebert at Tolbiac sealed their fate. Columbanus decided to go to Italy. His companion Gallus, one of the twelve who had come with him from Bangor, and who had been attacked by a fever, felt this new journey beyond his strength and refused to follow. Weak as Gallus was, Columbanus, whose faith would move mountains, did not forgive his old companion for once disobeying him; he forbade Gallus to say Mass as long as he himself was alive.

Columbanus and the others made for the Lombard duchy in Italy. Duke Agilolf was an Arian, but the duchess, Theudelinde, and her sons were Catholics. In the autumn of 612 the Irish monks crossed one of the Alpine passes which lead to Lake Maggiore and went as far as the Lombard capital, Milan. Here Columbanus soon became involved in theological disputes. Not only did Catholics and Arians oppose each other, but there was a split even in the Catholic camp. The latter was divided between the supporters and the opponents of the so-called Three Chapters, works by some extreme anti-Monophysites, which had been condemned by the Eastern Church at the request of the Emperor, Justinian, and, under pressure, also by Pope Vigilius in 547. The Catholics of Northern Italy had never accepted this condemnation which, as they knew perfectly well, had been wrested from the Pope. When, however, Gregory the Great had won over the Bishop of Milan and the Patriarch of Aquileia, while Theudelinde and the clergy of her court staunchly refused to follow suit, a dangerous rift had opened among the Catholics of Lombardy. In this situation Columbanus wrote a long letter to Pope Boniface IV. With all the rhetoric and imagery of which his language was capable Columbanus assured Boniface of his and his country's unfailing loyalty as he had assured Gregory; with the same candour as in his earlier letter he maintained that Vigilius had erred ("non bene vigilavit Vigilius" he says with a bitter pun) and that this error had had the most lamentable consequences.

BOBBIO

More than ever Columbanus, now in his seventies, longed for a quiet place of retreat. Duke Agilolf offered him the solitary site of Bobium (Bobbio) in the Apennines, where there was little more to be found than the ruins of an ancient church. Once more Columbanus undertook the work of founding a new monastery; his biographer tells us that he even joined in the work of building. He had been Abbot of Bobbio for only a few years when he died on 23 November, 615. He was succeeded by his beloved Attala, to whom he had written from Nantes in such great anxiety.

Bobbio's remote situation, and the long distance which separated it from its founder's native country, did not prevent the monastery from keeping in contact with Ireland, and in particular with the monastery of Bangor, from which Columbanus had come. Two ancient Bangor manuscripts, the famous Antiphonary and a Commentary on the Psalms with Old Irish glosses, seem to have found their way to Bobbio at an early date. The monks of Bobbio also made a collection of the writings of their founder.

As an author, Columbanus proves himself a master of every style in which he chose to write. His letters add a personal touch to this formal excellence. His Latin prose, in spite of classical echoes, is a product of its time. Such works as his Communal Rule and the greater part of his Penitential, which serve purely practical purposes, naturally lay no claim to literary (i.e. rhetorical) standards. In his Instructions, however—short sermons preached to his monks, probably at Milan—, he employs effectively a simple and almost naïve rhetoric. His *Regula Monachorum* impresses the reader by its unaffected and dignified tone—the style appropriate to religious instruction. The language and style of his letters vary according to situation and addressee. It is characteristic that in the first letter, addressed to Pope Gregory the Great, who was suspicious of the pagan classics, Columbanus makes next to no use of the rhetorician's art, but that in the fifth letter, written to Pope Boniface IV, he gives it free rein. In Letters II and IV, from which I have quoted, Columbanus speaks most personally, and with a directness behind which the stylist completely disappears.

The "humanism" of St. Columbanus, that is to say, his classical training and the effect which this training had on his mind and his style, is most evident in his poems. Only the poem on the Vanity of the World *(De Mundi Transitu)*, dating possibly from his Bangor days, is written in rhyming rhythmical lines. All the other poems are composed in classical metres, namely in the hexameter and the adonic. The latter is not used as a cadence after several longer lines as it was in classical times, but, in accordance with a common late Latin practice, as the unchanging metre of an entire poem—a practice of which the Irish would seem to have been particularly fond. The adonic work of Columbanus is an attractive piece of poetry. Its rather conventional theme, the dangers of great wealth, is for once treated in a fairly light vein, namely by telling stories from ancient mythology which prove the thesis. Among the hexametrical poems the Boating Song will probably have the greatest appeal to modern readers: the analogy of the rowers fighting against bad weather and of the soul fighting the devil arises spontaneously out of the situation and never becomes a stale allegory. The remaining two poems are moralizing in tone and are largely pieced together from lines and half-lines of classical poetry; they are valuable to us mainly as evidence of Columbanus's wide reading among the Latin poets, from the Augustan classics to his own time. Most conspicuous is his familiarity with Horace, who seems to have found no readers between Columbanus and the Irish scholars of the ninth century.

Although Bobbio and Luxeuil were in a sense daughter-houses of Bangor, they were by no means Irish monasteries like those at home. The monks in either place were recruited largely from the surrounding countryside. At Luxeuil, Columbanus's successor was a certain Eustasius, a native of Gaul. The first three abbots of Bobbio after Columbanus, Attala, Bertulf, and Bobolenus, have either German or Italian names. His biographer, Jonas, came from Northern Italy. As might be expected, Irish traditions were kept alive for some time. In Bobbio we can study the interplay of the Irish and the native elements in the manuscripts that were written there during the seventh and eighth centuries. Bobbio possessed also manuscripts that had come from outside. As early as the ninth century the library of that monastery became rich by the standards of those days. The activities of the Bobbio scriptorium are reflected vividly in a miscellaneous manuscript, now at Naples (Latinus 2, formerly Vienna Lat. 16). This codex contains some rare grammatical texts in a fluent fifth-century hand, probably Italian, beside grammatical and patristic texts in eighth-century Irish minuscule. The latter are partly written over deleted texts of late antiquity, among them fragments of the epic poem of Lucan and portions of a pre-Jerome Bible version. Bobbio once possessed numerous manuscripts of this type. They are technically called palimpsests, books in which the original text was deleted in order to make place for another text to be written over it. Bobbio, like Luxeuil, had a very poor start. Parchment was expensive, and the monks had often to be content with getting their writing material second-hand. During the invasions, many ancient manuscripts had been looted and had often suffered in the process. Yet other texts were no longer in demand. Such manuscripts came on the market as discards, and were sold at a "cut price". The monks availed themselves of this less expensive writing material; they deleted the original script as best they could, and wrote over it (more often either between the lines of the original, or across them) the texts of which they were in need. Luckily for us, they hardly ever succeeded in erasing the original text completely. In this way we have regained an almost complete edition of Plautus and a (fragmentary) copy of Cicero's *De Re Publica*, the only known copy of this important work. The manuscripts of Bobbio are at present widely scattered. A certain number of them are in the Vatican, others are in the University Library of Turin, but the largest portion was secured by Cardinal Federico Borromeo of Milan for his world-famous foundation, the Bibliotheca Ambrosiana.

Gallus, the "unfaithful" companion of Columbanus, had remained north of the Alps. When he had recovered from his illness, he retired into the wilderness on the banks of the River Steinach. There he lived, first as a hermit, later as the head of a small colony of monks, and preached the Christian message to the Alemanni, who for the greater part were still pagans. On his death-bed Columbanus bequeathed his staff to Gallus as a symbol of forgiveness, but Gallus (as legend has it) learnt about his master's death in a vision on the very night of his decease and said Mass for him on the following day. Of the later years of Gallus nothing is known for certain. His earliest "Life", of which only a fragment has survived, dates from the eighth century; the later ones, written by monks of Saint Gall and Reichenau (Wetti, Walahfrid Strabo, Notker Balbulus), are little more than stylistic improvements on the early one. Jonas of Bobbio, who knew Gallus personally, relates a story which he had from Gallus's own mouth: One day Columbanus sent Gallus to the River Breuchin near Luxeuil to fish. Gallus, an experienced fisherman, thought he knew better, and went instead to the River L'Ognon, where fish were more plentiful. Fish there were in abundance, but Gallus was not able to catch even a single one. In the evening Gallus came home with no catch at all. Columbanus reprimanded him for his disobedience, and sent him back to the River Breuchin, from which Gallus returned in no time, with a full net (I. 11). One wonders whether Jonas deliberately recorded Gallus's disobedience in a small matter but kept silent about his refusal to follow Columbanus into Italy.

The year of Gallus's death is unknown, but he must have died about the middle of the seventh century. About the year 720 the monastery of Saint Gall was founded on the site of Gallus's hermitage on the Steinach. It is probable, in spite of scanty documentation, that the place of Gallus's retreat was held in veneration from the time of his death, but there is no evidence to show that the hermitage continued without a break down to 720. Most of those who had gathered around Gallus in his lifetime were probably not Irish. It is therefore not surprising to see that during the first hundred years of the new abbey the Irish element was anything but strong. Those eighth-century scribes of Saint Gall whom we know by name, such as Liutfrid and Winithar, were Alemanni. The style of writing which developed at Saint Gall and in nearby Reichenau is called Alemannic. About the middle of the ninth century, however, the school of Saint Gall came under direct Irish influence. This episode is best described in the words of Ekkehard IV, in his continuation of Ratpert's *Casus Sancti Galli*:

At the time when Grimald was canonical abbot (841–872) and Hartmot his vice-gerent, we had the visit of an Irish bishop, Marcus. He was returning from Rome, and wished to visit the tomb of his fellow-countryman, St. Gall. With him was Moengal, his sister's son, whom afterwards we used to call by a diminutive form of his uncle's name, Marcellus. Moengal was very learned in sacred as well as profane knowledge. We elected Marcus's nephew a member of our community and asked the bishop to stay with us for some time. After long hesitation both, reluctantly, accepted our offer. On a stated day Marcellus, from his window, distributed a considerable portion of his uncle's money among their companions, for fear they might attack and maltreat him; for they thought he had persuaded his uncle to stay, and they took it badly. The bishop gave his horses and mules to some of his people whom he mentioned by name, but he retained his books, his gold, and his garments for himself and for St. Gall. After this, wearing his stole, he blessed those of his companions who wished to go home and bade them farewell; both sides parted with many tears. The bishop and his nephew stayed, together with some servants who spoke their language. After some time Marcellus was made head of the monastic school; among his pupils were Notker and some others who, then still being boys, entered the monastery about that time.

This is by no means the only reference to Moengal's activity in Saint Gall. He might, among other things, have been instrumental in initiating the great development of music in which Saint Gall took the lead. Between the years 853 and 860 Moengal wrote several deeds; in these he uses the Continental minuscule, not the Irish script. The manuscripts, however, which Marcus retained and which afterwards fell to the monastery were almost certainly the products of Irish scriptoria. A ninth-century manuscript of Saint Gall contains a list of *Libri Scottice scripti*, but it is impossible to decide whether this list, either wholly or in part, is identical with that of Bishop Marcus's books. The famous Saint Gall Gospels (Codex 51), one of the later representatives of Irish illuminative art, which dates from about 800, is not mentioned in that list. Some Irish manuscripts, however, had come to Saint Gall much earlier, and one or the other might have come from the saint in person. As early as the middle of the eighth century a Saint Gall scribe, possibly Liutfrid, made an attempt at imitating Irish minuscule; the result of his endeavour is preserved in Codex 213. It was not until the ninth century, however, that Saint Gall became one of the foremost centres of Irish culture on the Continent. At that time, in all probability, Dorbbéne's copy of Adamnán's *Life of St. Columba* (now Schaffhausen Gen. 1) arrived in the Reichenau district. In the Stiftsbibliothek of Saint Gall there are to the present day numerous manuscripts which testify to the monastery's role as mediator between Ireland and the Continent. Most important among these are some fragments of Irish liturgy and a copy of the Latin grammar of Priscian (Codex 904) with Irish glosses.

Ornamented initial from Priscian's Grammar at St. Gall.

THE GROWING SEED

WE have seen how Columba and Columbanus in their voluntary exile combined monastic asceticism with pastoral and missionary work and with the religious training of men who would continue what they had begun. While the Irish expansion in England had come to a halt after Whitby, the activities of Irish missionaries on the Continent or of men who had come under the influence of the Irish mission began to gather momentum just about the middle of the seventh century. In Merovingian France this expansion benefited considerably by the union of the several kingdoms under Clothar II (613) and by the prosperity of the realm under him and his son Dagobert I. The Irish found a powerful protector in Pipin, the mayor of the palace of Austrasia, and also enjoyed the support of some members of his family. Even in the time of St. Columbanus links between the Frankish nobility and the Irish had been established. A nobleman named Chagneric had sent his son Chagnoald to Luxeuil for his education. Columbanus's pupil ended his days as Bishop of Laon, and his sister Burgundofara founded the monastery of Faremoutiers. A prosperous member of the landed gentry in Picardy, Richarius, RICHARIUS renounced the world in response to the preaching of two Irishmen, led henceforth a life of severe mortification, and founded a monastery which still bears his name—Saint-Riquier. This is the story of his conversion:

Even at an early age blessed Richarius gave proof of a bright and lively mind.... Fichori and Chaidoc came from Ireland to France. When blessed Richarius first met them, the heathens of Ponthieu were just about to rise against them because they, in their ignorance, thought these men were sorcerers. The unbelievers called them evil spirits and charged them with the spiriting away of their crops. But the Lord, who knows everything before it comes to pass and manifests everything, chose his servant Richarius to deliver them from the hands of those ignorant people. He invited the servants of God, who as wayfarers had a special claim to hospitality, into his house. They gave thanks to God, who in His providence had sent them a man to rescue them from the insults of the ignorant and, out of charity, to offer them the safe refuge of his abode.

The whole night these servants of God preached the Gospel to Richarius. He listened to them, accepted the word of God, and confessed his sins with tears. From that day unto his death he lived as a penitent according to the holy precepts of religion.

Richarius died in about 645. Some years later (648) Wandregisil founded the abbey of Fontenelle (later named Saint-Wandrille after him) south of Rouen. Wandregisil, a count palatine, had a dream in which an angel took him to Bobbio and showed him the life of its monks. The count was so deeply impressed that he left the world and lived as an ascetic according to the Irish tradition; he died in an aura of sanctity, in 667 or 668. His friend Dado, a high officer at the court of Dagobert I, and his brothers, who in their youth had been blessed by St. Columbanus, founded a monastery of Irish character at Rebais near Paris in about 635. Five years later Dado was made Bishop of Rouen. A younger member of the same court circle, Philibert, founded the famous monastery of Jumièges about 655—another foundation of Irish character, as is proved by numerous copies of Hiberno-Latin texts which were written there and which are now in the public library of Rouen.

The life and work of such men as these bears witness to the impact which the powerful personality of St. Columbanus had had on the minds of the Franks. His example as a pioneer of Irish Christianity on the Continent was followed by great numbers of his fellow countrymen who left Ireland for the Frankish kingdoms.

DEICOLUS Deicolus is said to have been an Irish companion of Columbanus. His story is known only from a "Life" that dates from the tenth century. The saint might well have been Irish; his pious name ("Worshipper of God") could easily be a latinization of Dichul or Dic(h)uill. His legend tells some details which differ considerably from the well-known types of hagiographical cliché, and give the impression of being authentic. Deicolus began his "pilgrimage" in East Anglia, but later joined Columbanus. He was with him at Luxeuil and followed him into exile in 610. Poor health obliged him to stay behind in the Vosges, where he lived as a hermit. He used to spend long hours in prayer every night in a nearby chapel. The priest in charge of the chapel suspected the nightly visitor of some sexual crime and voiced his suspicion in public. When the lord of the demesne heard about this, he caused Deicolus to be castrated. Later, however, the hermit's innocence was established, and he was indemnified by the gift of a piece of land. There, on his own territory, Deicolus founded the monastery of Lüders (Lure). The false accusation and the undeserved punishment of Deicolus are probably a legendary "motif", but the remainder of his story fits well into the social pattern of his time. Deicolus is not given a piece of land for the purpose of building a church or monastery—a type of grant well-known all through the Middle Ages—but receives land as private property; as a landlord in his own right, like many a nobleman of those days, he founds a monastery on his estate.

FIACRIUS Another Irish name is that of Fiacrius (Fiachra). His "Life" is of even later date than that of Deicolus. Fiacrius chose for his retreat the Brie district, not far from Meaux, where Faro, a brother of Chagnoald and Burgundofara, was bishop. Fiacrius is believed to have built the first hostel for Irish pilgrims on the Continent and to have planted a kitchen garden from which to feed them.

FRIDOLIN Saint Fridolin too is supposed to have been Irish. His German name, which means "good companion", is not necessarily inconsistent with Irish nationality. Many Irish saints were known more widely by some name of endearment than by their real names, and if this was the case with Fridolin, his corresponding Irish name would have been changed to a German equivalent in his new surroundings. The "Life" of St. Fridolin, however, does not inspire credulity. It was written at the end of the tenth century by a certain Balther, a monk of Säckingen (in south-western Germany), which claimed Fridolin as its founder. Balther virtually admits that he knew nothing for certain about the saint whose life he set out to write. The story as we have it is also intrinsically untrustworthy. We are told that Fridolin came to Poitiers as early as 507, in the reign of Clovis I, the founder of the Merovingian dynasty, and that he restored there the church of the city's patron, St. Hilary, and gave to it the relics of that saint, which he had collected. Fridolin is then represented as moving farther eastward and as founding several monasteries on his way, among them Helera (now Eller on the Moselle) and Säckingen (on an island in the Rhine). The presence in France and Western Germany of an Irish pilgrim at the beginning of the sixth century is irreconcilable with the known history of that period. It is probable, however, that an Irishman named Fridolin belonged to the circle of Bishop Dido of Poitiers under Clovis II, about the middle of the seventh century. Dido, as we shall see later, had close links with Ireland.

About that time the Merovingian dynasty began to decline. Dagobert I (d. 639) was the last Merovingian king to rule over a united Frankish kingdom. After his death the country was again divided, and that division continued until Pipin of Heristal—as mayor of the palace, not as king—reunited the entire realm under his personal rule. Among the members of the royal family a woman was again outstanding—Bathild, the queen of Clovis II of Neustria. In 657 she invited monks from Luxeuil to found a new monastery, Corbie, on the River Somme in Picardy. She also founded a convent for nuns at Chelles near Paris; the nuns lived under a rule which had apparently been adapted from the rule of St. Columbanus. Corbie soon became an intellectual centre of the first order, which not only produced a great number of fine manuscripts (now for the greater part preserved at Amiens, Paris, and Leningrad) but also, especially during the eighth century, developed a series of characteristic writing styles. Chelles too, as Professor Bernhard Bischoff has pointed out recently, had some reputation as a writing centre, and specimens of this "nuns' minuscule" still survive.

In the course of the feuds which inevitably broke out again between the rulers of the rival kingdoms, the kings themselves as well as their respective mayors took great interest in the Irish monks who came to their shores, and gave them their protection. Both sides, it would seem, were anxious to enlist the moral support of the Irish *peregrini*, who by that time often enjoyed a reputation for sanctity and learning by the mere fact that they came from Ireland.

Against this background must be studied the activity of three brothers who, one after the other, travelled from Ireland via East Anglia to France, Saints Fursa, Foillan, and Ultan.

Best known among the three brothers is St. Fursa, the visionary. An account of his visions was given by Bede in his *Ecclesiastical History* (3, 19) and thus became widely known. The "booklet" to which Bede refers as his source is lost, but a Life of St. Fursa which was written before the end of the seventh century agrees so much with Bede's story that it probably represents his source in all essentials. From this document the following detail may here be quoted:

At one time there was a man of venerable manners, Furseus by name. He was of noble birth, but nobler still by his faith; renowned among his people according to worldly standards, yet more eminent because of the heavenly gift of grace. Even his infancy shone brightly in the light of wondrous prophecies. Under the care of holy priests and under the guidance of divine grace he was reared in the knowledge of Sacred Scripture and in the discipline of the cloister. He not only increased in years and in holy wisdom, but was also loved more and more every day by all those who knew him. He was handsome to look at, chaste, pious, friendly in conversation, attractive, prudent, moderate to an unusual degree, full of interior strength, unswerving in just judgement, long-suffering and generous, irresistible in his patience, of perfect humility, and filled with charitable solicitude for others. The flower of all virtue, which is wisdom, was his in such a high degree that, as the Apostle says, his word was always seasoned with the salt of grace.

Full of grace and rich in pious works, he left his native district and his father's house and spent several years studying Holy Scripture. When he had attained a sufficient knowledge of the Scriptures, he founded a monastery, where pious men gathered in great numbers. In his holy zeal he also prevailed on some of his relatives to join him there. With this end in view, he visited his home and family, and in spiritual conversation sowed the seed of the Sacred Word. There one day he fell ill. On the advice of some friends he moved to his paternal home. When he was already quite near the house and had just begun to recite devoutly the vesper psalms, he suddenly stopped as in complete darkness. His feet would no longer carry him. He was believed to be dead and was taken to the nearest house.

In this condition Fursa had those visions of the next world for which he was to become famous. These visions, like those of Tundalus and of Sir Owain (the first of many noblemen to visit St. Patrick's Purgatory), exercised a lasting influence on the medieval mind down to the time of Dante. Having had this vision, Fursa completely recovered.

He left the house, preached the word of God, and told the Irish what he had seen. There was grace in him beyond measure. He sought nothing that was of this world, he had time for everyone who approached him, high and low alike. Kings and nobles feared him, the humble and unworldly imitated him, all good people loved him, the wicked and the sinners trembled before him. The divine virtues shone forth from him. He expelled evil spirits from the bodies of their victims, and brought relief to the poor.

For one year he traversed Ireland in order to teach the people of his native island. As the anniversary of his vision drew near, he often said that he had been ordered to go on a day's journey. For in that night, when in the presence of many wise and holy men he had fallen so ill that hardly a spark of life was left in his breast, he (lifted, as it were, out of his body) had seen an angel who advised him about everything he was to preach later, and this angel had also told him that he would have to undertake a day's journey, and then to engage in the preaching of the Gospel for twelve years. And so it came to pass.

Ten years had already elapsed. Fursa preached the word of God without fear of anyone. He could no longer stand the crowds that flocked to him; he also suffered from the hostility of some people who envied him. He therefore left all that he owned behind and with some of his brethren retired to a small island in the sea. Shortly after this he crossed from Ireland to Wales and proceeded to the country of the Saxons. King Siggibercth received him honourably, and the heart of the barbarian was touched by the word of God.

When the twelve years of which the angel had spoken were over, Fursa, in an illness, saw again an angel in a vision. The angel exhorted him to preach with fervour. He foretold him nothing about the end of his life, nor did he reveal to him the day of his death; he merely reminded him of the word of the Gospel: Watch and pray, for ye know neither the day nor the hour (Mark 13.33). The man of God understood what the warning meant. He at once began to build a monastery in a place which he had been given by the king. This monastery was built in a fort named Cnoberesburg. It is situated in a lovely district, in the vicinity of forests and of the sea. The king of that people, Anna, and his nobles, donated the roof and made valuable presents.

All these things being duly completed, the man of God desired to retreat from all the cares of the world, and even from those concerning his monastery. He discussed his plan with some wise brethren, for he had in his community very wise and spiritual men who, inspired by his example, had proved themselves good monks and, by their daily toil, had won the grace of great progress in humility and charity. Among these were his brothers in the flesh: Foillan, a man of perfect sanctity, whom at his own departure he put in charge of the monastery and of the souls of its monks, and Ultan, whom after a long and perfect life with the community he had charged, years ago, to lead the life of a hermit. Leaving behind the world and all its worries, Fursa lived alone with his brother, who had already begun to lead a life of contemplation. Between daily work and constant prayer the two men spent one year together in holy wisdom.

Then, in an emergency, he was consulted by the king and the people as an inspired counsellor, or rather, he was urged to come to their aid. So he left his beloved solitude. Having weighed everything carefully in his mind, he realized that the province was threatened by an invasion of pagans (under King Penda of Mercia) and that monastic life had no chance of surviving there for long. He gave all the necessary advice and then set sail for Gaul. He was received with honour by King Chlodewech (Clovis II) of the Franks and by the patrician Ercanwald (Erchinoald, mayor of the palace of Neustria). Fursa founded a monastery in a place named Latiniacum (Lagny). A short time afterwards, when his brethren had already settled down in the new monastery, Fursa went on a journey together with the king and the patrician. On the way he fell ill. He lay low for many days. The nobles, and the king in person, who was much devoted to Fursa, paid him frequent visits. The words of grace that came from Fursa's lips gave the king a foretaste of the sweetness of eternal life. In this way Fursa left the world and entered into the everlasting kingdom.

His body was kept by the noble lord, the patrician Erchinoald, for burial in a church which he had just built with great splendour on his demesne of Péronne. The church was to be consecrated within thirty days. In the meantime the body was kept safe in a vault. At the end of that period the body was found intact, as if the saint had closed his eyes to the light of this world in that same hour. According to custom, he was buried reverently beside the altar, where he rested for four years. Then a chapel was built at the east side of the altar, and under the auspices of the venerable bishops Eligius (of Noyon) and Audoperth (of Cambrai) the body was transferred thither. Even after so many years it showed no symptoms of decay.

Fursa probably died either in 649 or in 650. His tomb at Péronne soon began to attract Irish pilgrims. The monastery which arose beside the tomb maintained close relations not only with Ireland in general but also with Fursa's family: his two brothers, first Foillan and later Ultan, held the abbacy there for some time. Throughout the eighth century, and possibly until its destruction by the Norsemen in 880, Peronna Scottorum preserved its Irish character.

Péronne was an important link between Ireland and the Continent also in the field of literature. Not only were some relics of St. Patrick deposited there, which Fursa had taken to France, but the monastery also possessed a text of Patrick's *Confession* and *Epistle*, which in all probability was the ancestor of the French and English copies of the *Libri Sancti Patricii*, and a Life of the saint, possibly Muirchú's. The cult of St. Patrick at Péronne is attested also by an inscription in Latin verse which Abbot Cellanus of Péronne (c. 700) composed for his church:

> *This hall perpetuates Saint Patrick's fame,*
> *Whom humbly we revere, as is his due.*
> *He bathed us in the sacramental bath,*
> *He taught us how to worship God in heaven,*
> *Bright'ning our darkness with the light of faith.*
> *Calpornius' son, in Britain he was born,*
> *Gaul reared him, happy Ireland gave him rest.*
> *Thus heaven's blessing shines on either land.*

The second and third last lines of this poetic inscription echo a type of ancient sepulchral epigram, which is best known to us from the epitaph of Virgil. Cellanus seems to have been a *littérateur* of some importance. He was an admirer of Aldhelm, with whom he exchanged letters. One of these letters, which has survived, shows Cellanus as a master of the same artificial prose style which had been affected by his admired model.

A daughter-house of Péronne was Fosses (near Nivelles) in Brabant. Its founder, Fursa's brother Foillan, had fled to Péronne with his entire community in about 650, when Penda of Mercia, the last pagan among the Anglo-Saxon kings, had attacked East Anglia and destroyed Cnoberesburg. At Péronne the exiles were offered asylum by Erchinoald. There was no accommodation, however, for settling a large monastic community in addition to the existing one. Thus Erchinoald, it would seem, suggested—politely, but in no uncertain terms—that the newcomers should look for some other place as their permanent home. They went to Nivelles, where Itta, the widow of Pipin I, was abbess of a nunnery. Under the patronage of Itta and of her brother Grimoald, mayor of the palace of Austrasia, Foillan founded the monastery of Fosses. The foundation falls before Itta's death in 652. Some years later (probably on 31 October, 655) Foillan was killed by robbers not far from Nivelles. The story of Foillan is known from a document which was composed shortly after his death.

After holy Furseus had left the country across the sea, the disaster which he had foreseen broke loose. The Christian king, Anna, was expelled, the heathens attacked the monastery which Fursa had built there, the monks and their property were scattered. Abbot Foillan himself, the saint's brother, was just being escorted to his execution when the hand of God saved him for the benefit of many. It was reported that King Anna had returned, and the heathens fled in terror. Foillan bought back his monks from slavery; and having found the relics of his monastery, its sacred vessels and books, he put everything on board a ship, which took him and his community to France. Erchinoald, who has been mentioned above, received the foreigners at the place where blessed Furseus had been buried. Soon afterwards, however, the patrician, who had no high opinion of these aliens, told them to move on. The pious servant of God Idoberga, surnamed Ita, and her daughter Gertrud, a virgin of Christ, gave them shelter. The lord Grimoald himself welcomed them, and founded for them a monastery on one of his estates, which is called Bebrona after the river which flows through it. Ita, the servant of God, provided the necessities of life.

There it happened, after the servant of God had died, … that the holy man Foillan, of whom we have spoken, had to go on a journey for the good of his flock. It was on the vigil of the feast of St. Quintinus the martyr (30 October). After the celebration of solemn Mass at the church of Nivelles Foillan asked the senior brethren that they, who had shared all his labours, should, in their charity, search for his body if he were to die on that journey. Then he bade farewell to all and went on his way. In that same night he was led astray by bad people. The hut to which he was guided was inhabited by evil men, who received him with feigned friendliness. His companions, who did not trust those people, kept awake all night. After Lauds had been recited, he addressed some kind words to the inhabitants of the hut, said a prayer, admonished his companions not to think evil of anybody, and went to sleep. Those devilish men, however, got up again and with the help of others whom they had brought along, they killed the holy man and his companions. The holy man exclaimed "Deo gratias"; they, however, for fear he might be heard, cut off his head. Then they dug a pit in an adjacent building where a herd of pigs was kept, and there, without fear of God, they disposed of the four bodies, which they had cut to pieces. The crime remained undiscovered for many days because the felons had taken the garments of their victims, the saint's horse, and all the belongings of the four persons outside the country and sold them there. When it became known, however, that the travelling party had not reached their destination, the brethren at home, in their charity, began to worry about them. They made a public announcement and had them searched for all over the country. The virgin of Christ, Gertrud, besought God with fasts and incessant prayer, and sent out speedy messengers in all directions. At last she succeeded in bringing the dark crime into the light of day. On the seventy-seventh day after the murder—a mystical number, which is found in many passages of Holy Scripture —the four bodies were discovered. It was on the anniversary of the day on which Foillan's brother, Saint Fursa, had passed away (16 January). The bodies were exhumed and, by the light of candles and torches, to the chanting of antiphons and spiritual hymns, were reverently carried to Nivelles on the shoulders of the clergy and people in a nocturnal procession. On the same day the venerable Dido, Bishop of Poitiers, and Grimoald, the mayor of the palace, had come to Nivelles in order to visit the holy place together. They were told by the Lord of the arrival of the holy bodies… The venerable bishop went out in a hurry to meet them; with many tears he prayed and gave glory to the Lord. Then he and the noble patrician Grimoald put the burden of the sacred body (of Foillan) on their shoulders and carried it. The body was first taken to the convent of the holy virgins, who received some relics; then, with psalms and canticles, it was carried to Foillan's own monastery. All the nobles went out to meet the procession, and (in turn) carried the body on their shoulders. It was deposited with great honour in the celebrated place (Bebrona) which is also called Fosses, where prayers are granted by the grace of our Lord Jesus Christ.

This account was written by an Irish-trained cleric of Nivelles at a time when St. Gertrud was still abbess, that is to say before December 658, when she resigned in favour of her niece Wulfetrude. The *terminus a quo*, as Père Grosjean suggests with great probability, is 16 January, 656. That the bodies were found on the feast of St. Fursa is stated expressly in the document itself. The year 656 is suggested by the presence of Dido and Grimoald. Père Grosjean suspects with good reason that the mayor of the palace and the bishop of Poitiers combined their pilgrimage to Nivelles with a discussion of high politics. Only a fortnight later King Sigebert III suddenly died at the early age of twenty-seven. Grimoald forced the young prince, Dagobert II, to become a monk, and Dido, into whose care the novice was given, soon afterwards sent him away to Ireland. In his stead Grimoald's own son, Childebert the Adopted, was raised to the throne of Austrasia. This was the first attempt on the part of the family later known as the Carolingians to put the man who actually held power in the place of a king who ruled only in name. The *coup d'état*, however, had no lasting success. Either in the same or in the following year Grimoald's power was broken, and Clovis II of Neustria ordered his execution. Grimoald's son Childebert maintained himself as king of Austrasia until his death in 662, but with Childeric II, who once more united Austrasia and Neustria, the Merovingians returned to the throne of Austrasia. When Childeric was murdered, chaos reigned again for some time; by the intervention of Wilfrid of York, even Dagobert was allowed to come home from Ireland as a pretender. Finally Grimoald's nephew, Pipin II, emerged as mayor of the palace of a united Frankish kingdom and thus in actual fact as sole ruler. The early contacts of this great dynasty with an Irish saint and founder of monasteries is not without historical significance.

The third brother, Ultan, was active in the same circle. At some time, which cannot be exactly determined, he was Abbot of Péronne, and after Foillan's death he became Abbot of Fosses. He is said to have foretold to St. Gertrud on the day before her death that she would go to heaven on the following day, which was the feast of St. Patrick. St. Gertrud died on 17 March, 659. The earliest Life of this saint, written by an Irishman at Nivelles in about 670, is one of the oldest monuments of Irish hagiography.

The alleged Irish origin of some other Belgian saints is doubtful. In the case of St. Dympna, patroness of Gheel near Antwerp, a genuine tradition to that effect cannot be ruled out. Much stronger doubts must be entertained as regards St. Romuald of Malines. He is said to have been Bishop of Dublin before leaving his country, but for all that we know Dublin did not become an episcopal see before the eleventh century. Livinus, patron of Ghent, may not even be a historical character, but merely a doublet of the Anglo-Saxon Lebuin, who preached at Deventer in Holland during the eighth century. The Lives of all these saints are of late date and have little, if any, historical value. At the time of their composition the fame of Ireland as the Island of Saints was a temptation for any hagiographer to represent his hero as an Irishman.

Another of these pseudo-Irish saints, probably, is Pirmin (d. c. 754), who founded the famous island monastery of Reichenau in Lake Constance. The question of his origin has not yet been settled, but it seems most likely that he was a native of Spain. From the ninth century onwards, however, the monastery of Reichenau counted among its monks many who were Irish, and the remnants of its library (now for the greater part at the Badische Landesbibliothek in Karlsruhe) include a very considerable number of manuscripts and fragments of manuscripts in the Irish script, some also in the Irish language. PIRMIN

Thuringia and Eastern Franconia were converted by an Irish preacher named Kilian, who suffered martyrdom, together with his two companions Kolonat and Totnan, near Würzburg about the year 689. The relics of the apostles of Franconia were found in 752 and were given to the newly-founded cathedral of Würzburg by Burchardt, whom St. Boniface had consecrated first bishop of that city. Pipin the Short, since 751 King of the Franks, gave the new see his special protection. Soon St. Kilian's tomb was visited by numerous pilgrims from his native country. His cult was attested in the late eighth century, but the two "Passiones" of the saint and his companions, neither of which is free from legendary elements, are a century later. As might be expected in a cathedral town connected with the mission of St. Boniface, Würzburg in its early years was dominated by Anglo-Saxon influence. With the visits of Irish pilgrims, however, ties with Kilian's native country became stronger. A famous Irish scholar, Clemens Scottus, who had been head of the palace school under Louis the Pious, and tutor of the emperor's son, Lothar, apparently died there, possibly as a pilgrim to St. Kilian's tomb. It is now generally believed that some of the Irish manuscripts at Würzburg, for example the Epistles of St. Paul with Irish glosses and the Gospel of St. Matthew with glosses and commentary (Mp. th. f. 61), were brought to the famous shrine by Irish visitors during the ninth century. Another Würzburg manu- KILIAN script of St. Paul, with a crucifixion which is often reproduced (f. 69), may be called Irish only in an indirect sense. This miniature, either directly or through a mediator, merely reproduces an earlier Irish original. The text is written in an Anglo-Saxon hand, probably of the Würzburg area, of about 800. As a localized group, the ancient manuscripts of Würzburg, beside those of Reichenau, are our most valuable evidence of the influence of insular culture on the nascent spiritual and intellectual life of Germany.

Devotion to St. Kilian probably accounts also for the fact that Würzburg became the seat of one of the earliest *Schottenklöster* in Germany. Although we hear nothing about Irish pilgrims at Würzburg for a long time after the end of the ninth century, a new wave of pilgrims is attested in about the middle of the eleventh century, and we are probably correct in the assumption that this pilgrimage was never completely abandoned. Eminent among eleventh-century pilgrims were the two Mariani Scotti, the chronicler (who spent some time as an *inclusus* at Fulda and Mayence) and the founder of Weih-Sankt-Peter at Ratisbon. Both had a great devotion to St. Kilian; the former had been ordained (1059) at St. Kilian's tomb.

Slowly but surely the work of Irish missionaries was absorbed in the ecclesiastical organization of Germany which had been established with such great zeal and energy by St. Boniface. The case of Würzburg is typical. A late offshoot of the Irish mission is found in the south-east of Germany, where an Irishman was active towards the end of the eighth century. Here, however, a conflict arose which is reminiscent of the Roman-Celtic controversy of earlier times. It is the story of Bishop Arbeo of Freising and of his Irish neighbour, Bishop Virgil of Salzburg.

In 765 Arbeo had opened the tomb of St. Corbinian, the apostle of Bavaria and first bishop of Freising, and had brought the saint's body to his cathedral. Some years later Arbeo wrote a Life of this saint. Whether Corbinian was Irish remains uncertain. His name is Celtic, but he might have been a native of the Alps, possibly of the Vintschgau, where he had been buried. Arbeo mentions in passing the fact that Corbinian was believed to be British. To a man reared in the strict Roman tradition of Boniface's Germany as was Arbeo, the epithet "Celtic" was by no means one of distinction. And yet, as a writer, Arbeo is not in the Anglo-Saxon tradition of Aldhelm or Bede, but under the strong influence of the Irishman Virgil. And not only was Virgil his stylistic model, he also had urged Arbeo to write the Life of Corbinian. Arbeo acknowledged his debt of gratitude by dedicating his work to the Bishop of Salzburg.

VIRGIL   Virgil (the name is probably a Latinization of the Irish Fergil) had left his country in about 742. In the following year he was at the court of Pipin, then still mayor of the palace. The learned man, to whom Irish annalists refer as "the geometer", greatly impressed Pipin; two years later, with Pipin's special recommendation, Virgil was sent to Duke Odilo of Bavaria, who put the Irishman in charge of the vacant see of Salzburg. However, Virgil soon aroused the suspicions of the Primate of Germany. The details are known from two letters of Pope Zacharias to Boniface. The first one (dated 1 July, 746—or 744?) is the Pope's reply to an order of Boniface to repeat the baptism of a number of Virgil's converts. Boniface held that in their cases baptism had been administered invalidly, but the Pope, on the grounds of a report which he had received from Virgil and his companion Sidonius (later Bishop of Passau), decided for the validity of the act in those cases. A new clash occurred some years later. On the authority of some ancient cosmographers, Virgil had asserted the existence of antipodes, and Boniface, who thought this opinion was contrary to the teaching of the Church, had informed the Pope of Virgil's alleged heresy. Pope Zacharias's answer deserves to be quoted in full:

(Pope Zacharias to Archbishop Boniface, 1 May, 748:)

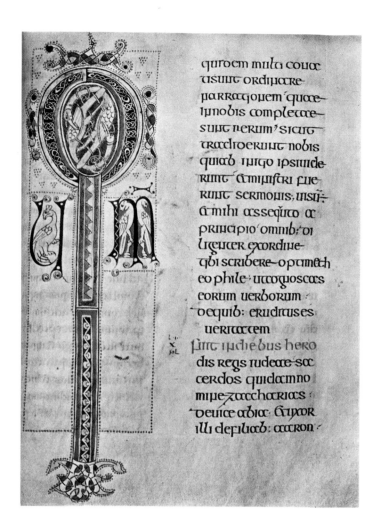

quioem multa conac
usunt ordinare
narragonem quae
lunobis compleccae
sunt nerum sicut
tradioerunt nobis
quiab inirio ipsunide
runt commissri fue
runt sermonis insu
cc mihi cssequto cc
principio omnib, oi
licencer exordine
qbi scribere opumech
eo phile uccogoscas
eorum uerborum
oequib, erudicuses
ueritaccem
sinc indiebus hero
dis regis iudeae sac
cerdos quidamno
mine zacchacrias,
deuice abia, crixor
illi defiliab, aacron,

Fol. III R of the Cutbercht Gospels in the
National Library, Vienna.

*Of this also your brotherly holiness has informed us that the said Virgil... speaks ill of you because you have
blamed him for a deviation from Catholic doctrine. He gives Otilo, the Duke of Bavaria, no peace, in order to
sow hostility between you and him. He further asserts that, with my consent, he holds the see of one of those four
brethren, now deceased, whom you, my dear brother, have consecrated bishops. There is no truth whatsoever in
this assertion, malice has lied against itself (Psalm 26.12). As regards the perverse and evil doctrine which he
is said to have put forth against God and his own soul: if it is established as certain that he holds that opinion,
namely that there is another world under this world, with other people, another sun and another moon, then con-
vene a synod, expel him from the Church, and suspend him from the exercise of his priestly office. In the meantime We Ourselves have written to the said duke, and through the latter have summoned the said Virgil to
appear before Us so that, if he be found to be in error, he may be punished according to the canonical sanctions.
For those who sow grief will harvest grief (John 4.8).*

The Pope thus adopted an attitude of prudent non-commitment with regard to Virgil's alleged
heresy, but denied categorically Virgil's claim that he held the diocese of Salzburg with the Pope's
consent. Here we are at the root of the conflict. It is known that Virgil administered the affairs of the
Salzburg diocese not as bishop but as abbot of St. Peter's, and that all episcopal functions were exercised
by an Irish bishop, Dobdagrecus (that is, Dub-dá-chrich), who was a monk of his monastery. This
"Celtic" irregularity could not possibly be tolerated by the organizer of the Roman Church in

Germany. Virgil, however, must have been in a very strong position. Of his "heretical" cosmography we hear no more; it may be taken for granted that Virgil in some way made his peace with the ecclesiastical authorities. He did, however, continue to govern the diocese of Salzburg as a mere abbot for nearly another twenty years. In 767 at long last, at the urgent request of his fellow-bishops, he consented to receive episcopal consecration. That Virgil maintained relations with Ireland, and especially with Iona, all his life is proved by the Confraternity Book of St. Peter's, Salzburg. After a long life of fruitful labour, in particular as missionary among the Slavs of Carinthia, Virgil died in 784. He was succeeded by Arno, a pupil of Alcuin.

Virgil was a man of wide intellectual interests. His epithet "the geometer" suggests that he took some interest in science (the "quadrivium" as it was then called), which was rather exceptional in his time. His special subject apparently was cosmography. He was of course familiar with the writings of the Fathers and with the encyclopedic literature of late antiquity. It was probably under his abbacy that Salzburg acquired the beautifully illumined Gospel manuscript (now Vienna 1224), which an eighth-century Anglo-Saxon—apparently on the Continent—named Cutbercht had written.

The full stature of Virgil the writer has been revealed only recently, when the German historian Heinz Löwe brilliantly proved that the cosmography of the so-called Aethicus Ister is actually a work of Virgil of Salzburg. This cosmography, conceived ostensibly in the tradition of Irish travel literature on the one hand and of the philosophical romances of late antiquity on the other, is a strange mixture of interesting information concerning north-west Europe and of the most fantastic cosmographical fables. It parades as the work of an Istrian "philosopher", that is to say, a pagan *savant*, edited (and censored in the process) by St. Jerome. However, linguistic peculiarities and some of the subject-matter point to an Irishman as author, and the fact that Arbeo in his Life of St. Corbinian unmistakably imitates the style of "Aethicus Ister"—the earliest (eighth-century) manuscript of which was written at Freising—is strongly suggestive of the authorship of Virgil, to whom, as we have seen, Arbeo's work was dedicated. In the assumed double part of Jerome as "editor" and Aethicus as "author" one can hardly help seeing a reflection of the controversy between Virgil and Boniface. The subtle satire, perhaps deliberately obscured for undiscriminating readers, which consists in the serving up of absurd fables to the exponents of an excessive traditionalism on the unsuspected authority of a great patristic name, had the effect of mystifying not only Arbeo, who apparently took it on good faith, but many generations after him. Virgil the cosmographer, having renounced his belief in the antipodes, would thus have had his revenge, in true Irish fashion, by pulling his opponent's leg.

If not all that was told later about Irish monks and bishops on the Continent of Europe stands up to historical criticism, it is, on the other hand, beyond doubt that our explicit sources for the activity of the Irish in France and in the neighbouring countries tell considerably less than the full story. Recent studies of "insular symptoms" in Continental script, illumination, and "book technique", of the Irish element in literature, of the give-and-take between Irish and Continental liturgy, which differ so fundamentally in attitude, have made us realize more and more that the cultural emanation from such centres as Luxeuil, Bobbio, Péronne, or the Irish-Northumbrian Echternach must have gone far beyond the facts for which there is direct evidence, and that these centres, though of special importance, cannot have been the only points of contact between insular and continental culture. It is hardly an exaggeration to say that between 600 and 750 the Irish—first alone and later together with the Anglo-Saxons—constitute the decisive cultural factor throughout the territory of the future Carolingian Empire. It was, for all that we know, the Irish who first brought to Central Europe the works of the last great universal writer in the ancient tradition, Isidore of Seville (d. 636). We still

Opposite:
Opening page of the Gospel according to St. Matthew:
XPI AUTEM GENERATIO..., in the Gospels of St. Chad in the Library of Lichfield Cathedral.

104

possess a fragment of Isidore's *Etymologiae* in an archaic Irish minuscule, which might have been written in Isidore's lifetime or, at the latest, shortly afterwards; it is preserved in Saint Gall (cod. 1399. a. 1). That Isidore was studied in the Irish schools as early as the seventh century is well known. Even when the Anglo-Saxon mission was in full swing the Irish were still prominent in the field of learning; only the Northumbrians could rival them. The intellectual interests of Boniface and his circle were rather limited. Anglo-Saxon learning did not fully mature before Alcuin, who had studied in Northumbrian York, partly under Irish teachers.

The greatest impact the Irish had was in the field of religion. The rigorous asceticism of the Irish monks, compared to which the rule of St. Benedict must have appeared soft, not only inspired individuals like Richarius or Wandrigisil, but also attracted many a native of France and Italy to the Columban monasteries of Annegray, Luxeuil, and Bobbio. Luxeuil gave its rule to Corbie. There, however, as in most other Irish foundations, it was gradually superseded by the less exacting rule of St. Benedict. Only Péronne, as far as we can see, preserved its Irish character to the last. The Columban rule became the model for other rules, for example for the rule of Columban's disciple Donatus, and for a nuns' rule which is known from the collection of rules made by Benedict of Aniane. Irish penitential discipline spread even more widely. Irish penitentials or penitentials modelled on Irish ones were copied frequently down to the end of the tenth century. It is hardly accidental that the Penitential of Vinnian had been preserved at Salzburg and Saint Gall, that of Columbanus at Bobbio, and that a number of similar texts, coupled with the *Collectio Canonum Hibernensis* (an Irish collection of synodal acts, made early in the eighth century), had their centre of distribution in Brittany. The range of influence becomes still wider if we consider the effect these compilations had on genuinely continental ones. The Penitential of Columbanus forms the basis of many a Frankish work of this kind, and that of Cummean was used so extensively in the *Capitula Iudiciorum* and in the Saint Gall *Paenitentiale Tripartitum* that the original text, which is badly transmitted, can largely be restored by the help of its derivatives. In this field, too, the Anglo-Saxon "superstructure" is present. A number of penitentials combine Cummean with Pseudo-Theodore, in particular the so-called *Excarpsus Cummeani*, which was widely distributed from the eighth century onwards. Penitentials of pure Anglo-Saxon origin also were known and copied on the Continent. These texts, attributed to Theodore of Tarsus, Bede, and Egbert respectively, in spite of an anti-Celtic tendency, testify to the influence of the Irish penitential system even in the English Church of the time. They do, however, modify the Irish practice, and—as is evident from "Theodore"—are reluctant to accept the principle of "commutation" *(arreum)*.

The influence of the Irish liturgy on that of the Continent presents a more difficult problem. The early Irish liturgy, which was abandoned for the Roman one during the eleventh century, is only fragmentarily known. The interpretation of Irish liturgical texts must also take into account the fact that the Irish liturgy is the isolated development of an early form of the Gallican liturgy of Gaul, and that parallels between Irish and Gallican liturgical texts may be the result of either their common origin or later influence of the one on the other. An early Gallican origin of the Irish liturgy is suggested by, among other things, the Irish word for "Mass"—*oifrend*, from Latin *offerenda*, which in the Ambrosian liturgy is the word for "offertory". The canon of the Mass in the "Stowe Missal" (now in the Royal Irish Academy), the only manuscript with a purely Irish missal text, written about the year 800, is, however, the "Gelasian" canon, which differs but little from the "Gregorian" canon of the present Roman Missal, and on a page of the Book of Armagh (c. 807) we read the *Hanc igitur* prayer in the enlarged form which it was given by Gregory the Great. When faced with a Continental Irish manuscript such as the "Bobbio Missal" (so called because Dom Mabillon discovered it at

Opposite:
Crucifixion on fol. 38 of Codex A. II. 17 of the Cathedral Library, Durham.

Bobbio in 1686), a manuscript written probably in south-eastern France during the eighth century, the liturgist is still puzzled. That the Irish liturgy was eclectic, that is to say, that it combined Gallican, Mozarabic, and later also Roman elements, is common knowledge. It is characteristically Irish to have so few texts for special Masses *(missae propriae)*, a feature also of Eastern liturgies. In this respect the "Stowe Missal" is an extreme case. It has only three Masses: one for the feasts of saints, one for penitents on earth, and one for the dead. Normally Mass was celebrated only on Sundays, and the mass text was that of Easter, each Sunday participating in the paschal mystery. The "cyclic" concept of time which underlies this liturgical attitude—to use a formulation of John Hennig—and which is in strong contrast to the "linear historical" concept of liturgical time prevalent on the European Continent, determines also the Irish form of devotion to the saints. Continental churches from early times celebrated the *Natalis*, that is, the day of the saint's death, as his heavenly birthday. The anniversary of the *Natalis* of each individual saint was observed liturgically year after year by a special mass text and a special choir office. There also existed Martyrologies, which gave for each day of the year the names of the martyrs and other saints who had died on that day but were not otherwise liturgically commemorated. In Ireland all the saints (represented by their several categories) were remembered at every Mass; they were also invoked by name in long litanies. There were, however, no feasts of individual saints to mark the anniversary of their deaths, but only a common feast of all the saints. As a parallel it may be remarked here that in ancient Ireland church dedications to saints were also unknown. It was probably not long before 800 that the Martyrology was brought to Ireland. From that time onwards, after the analogy of the continental practice, "feasts" of Irish saints were entered in martyrologies under the calendar dates of their obits. This is the case in the Martyrology of Tallaght (ninth century) and in the "Calendar" (Féilire) of Oengus the Culdee (c. 800). The latter is written in Irish verse, each stanza containing the names of "Roman" and Irish saints for one day of the year, with characteristic epithets. The author, according to John Hennig, did not intend to versify a liturgical martyrology but composed a religious poem, based on the martyrology, which could be recited at one reading as a form of private devotion to all the saints. Irish liturgy, like Irish art, has always accepted foreign influences as a stimulus, translating them into its own native idiom. In Ireland the day when St. Donnan and his companions, the only martyrs of the Irish Church at home, died on the island of Eig off the Scottish coast (Easter Sunday, 17 April, 617—the feast day, according to the Roman calendar, of the martyr Peter the Deacon) was celebrated as the Feast of All the Saints of Europe—the first instance of an All Hallows Day. There is reason for believing that the Feast of All Saints on the 1st of November is also of Irish origin.

Communities of Irish monks on the Continent would cling to their liturgy as they clung to other customs of their own Church. In many other ways they were able to contribute something new to the religious life in their adopted countries. The liturgical traditions of the Continent, however, were too strong. As early as the seventh century the Gelasian Sacramentary had been introduced in France, and during the eighth the Gallican liturgy was for the greater part dying out except for those elements which had become incorporated in the later Gelasianum. When at last Charlemagne obtained from Pope Hadrian a standard text of the Gregorian Sacramentary, into which Alcuin incorporated certain Gallican elements, this Gallico-Roman missal was prescribed for the churches of the entire Frankish realm. It has remained the basis of the Roman Missal to the present day. The Irish liturgy, which was so much less developed, could not rival the Roman liturgy of France. In the more intimate sphere of private devotion, however, Irish practices were introduced and imitated. Literary evidence to this effect is the *Martyrologium Poeticum* of Wandelbert of Prüm (about the middle of the ninth century), a work which could not have been produced without some knowledge, either direct or indirect, of

Féilire Oengusso or similar Irish productions. By the very existence of such a poem it is suggested that the Irish devotion to all saints had found its way to the Continent. Continental manuscripts contain also some of the Latin hymns of the Irish Church, although there are no collections as rich as the Antiphonary of Bangor or the Irish *Liber Hymnorum* (in two recensions, eleventh and twelfth century). These hymns, however, do not seem to have been used liturgically on the Continent as they were in Ireland.

Reliquary of St. Patrick's bell, made of bronze, and ornamented with gold, silver, and enamels. 11th century. National Museum, Dublin.

Wherever the Irish went they brought with them the fame of their native saints. Their continental converts and disciples were fascinated by these strange figures, who according to legend had led lives full of fantastic miracles, and took to them with enthusiasm. They added their cult to that of their own traditional saints, but gave it the form to which they were accustomed from the cult of their own martyrs and confessors and of those Irish saints who had lived and laboured among them. More and more often ecclesiastical calendars list the feasts of Irish saints, and not only those of the continental mission field but also those of the homeland, under their real or supposed *Natalis*. The day of St. Patrick's death is found for the first time in a continental source, the Life of St. Gertrud of Nivelles, who had died on St. Patrick's Day, 17 March. Of continental origin also are the earliest liturgical offices of Irish saints, but there is evidence to show that some of them came to Ireland at a fairly early date. The earliest instance on record is the mention made of an *Offertorium proprium* for St. Patrick's Day in the Book of Armagh by the *scriba* Ferdomnach, whose activity is attested for the period 807 to 845.

There is further evidence of the spreading of the cults of Irish saints in the peregrinations of their written Lives. The national triad of saints, Patrick, Brigit, and Columcille, as well as Brendan the Navigator, are frequently represented in continental Legendaria, collections of Lives of saints which from the tenth century onward were compiled on an ever-increasing scale. It goes without saying that besides the saints of the homeland these Legendaria normally contain also Lives of the great Irish missionaries, Columbanus, Gallus, Fursa, Kilian and others, and of their disciples. Muirchú's Life of St.Patrick was copied by an Anglo-Saxon scribe on the Continent as early as the eighth century; it was probably at Péronne even in the time of Cellanus. Texts depending on a later, and more comprehensive, Life of St.Patrick testify to its journeying through northern France, the Ardennes, the Rhine valley, and Bavaria into Austria. A Life of St.Brigid was copied in western Germany about the middle of the ninth century, and the Life of the same saint by Cogitosus was known in France during the tenth century (if not earlier) and in southern Italy during the eleventh. Adamnán's Life of St.Columba had reached Alemannia in the ninth century; the earliest continental copy of that text (Saint Gall, Codex 555) was made probably under Abbot Grimald. The Brendan legend is attested in Brittany in the ninth century, and at Trèves in the tenth, where the earliest extant manuscript of the *Navigatio* was written. The text might have been brought to Trèves by Bishop Israel Brittigena. From Trèves the text was taken to Ratisbon, where it is listed in a library catalogue of St.Emmeran of the year 994.

These much and widely read texts could not fail to influence continental hagiography as regards both content and form. In the absence of detailed comparative studies this process can be described only summarily. One particular type of miracle, however, namely that in which a saint hangs his or her wet garment on a sunbeam to dry, has plausibly been derived from a story in the Legend of St. Brigit. In a more general way the Lives of Irish saints by continental biographers (some are as early as the seventh century) and the Lives of continental saints written in an Irish milieu are invariably pervaded by the spiritual atmosphere of Irish Christianity. An Irish "symptom" is also the frequent assertion that a saint was of royal blood. In Ireland, where there existed about a hundred small tribal kingdoms, and where the monasteries had such close links with the ruling families of the several *tuatha*, saints of royal descent were by no means rare.

The literary baggage of Irishmen travelling on the Continent was not confined to Lives of Saints. They imported also their Latin writings on theology and on those learned disciplines which were studied in their schools. We know this Hiberno-Latin literature of the seventh and eighth centuries almost exclusively from continental and later English copies. The lack of manuscripts preserved in Ireland is largely the result of the Viking invasions and of the later history of Ireland, which was a long series of destructive wars and upheavals. Were it not for the interest which continental scholars took in this literature from the eighth century onwards, it would have been lost almost entirely. The distribution pattern of manuscripts in which these texts are preserved shows clearly that their dissemination started from the great Irish centres on the Continent, from Luxeuil and Bobbio, Péronne, Corbie, Jumièges, Saint Gall and Reichenau, Salzburg, and Freising. In some cases the entire continental tradition of a text is derived from a single exemplar. For example, the numerous manuscripts of Adamnán's work *On the Holy Places* have all at one point a badly corrupted text, and the only possible explanation of the corruption is this: that a continental scribe misunderstood the unfamiliar *signes de renvoi* of his exemplar, which indicated an omission supplied in the margin. Some Latin writings of Irish origin owe their popularity in the first place to the fact that they circulated under the name of a famous patristic writer such as Cyprian, Jerome, or Augustine. Best known among these texts is the tract *On the Twelve Abuses of the World*, of which there exist hundreds of copies in manuscript down to the end of the Middle Ages. Such Pseudo-Patristica were produced also in Irish centres on the Continent. Two of these, which go under the name of St.Isidore, namely the *Liber de Numeris* and a recension of the *Liber de Ortu et Obitu Patrum*, were produced in the circle of Virgil of Salzburg.

Besides their own literary productions the Irish and Anglo-Saxons on the Continent were instrumental also in the transmission of theological and other scholastic literature not of insular origin.

The "seven churches" of Inishmore in the Aran Islands.

Numerous texts of all kinds are known from manuscripts in insular script or in continental script which in its ductus, its abbreviation, and its style of ornamentation betrays insular influence. To study these influences in detail is one of the most fascinating tasks of the palaeographer and the art historian.

The Chalice of Ardagh, seen from the side and from below. National Museum, Dublin.

All the more puzzling is the almost complete absence of Irish influence on continental art in other fields than that of book illumination. The late seventh and the eighth century is the golden age of Celtic art in Ireland. It is the period of the Tara Brooch, the communion chalice of Ardagh, the Moylough bronze and silver reliquary for a belt, and besides these works in metal and enamel we have carved crosses with ornamentation and figures like that of Ahenny in Co. Tipperary. Of such works there is hardly a trace on the Continent. It is true that Irish monasteries on the Continent started off being very poor, and that later, when they had become wealthy, Carolingian civilization had developed an eclectic art of its own, and one of great technical perfection. This explanation, however, hardly accounts for everything. Equally strange is the comparative lack of representative works of book illumination in the mother country. Admittedly, it must not be forgotten that the place of origin of the Book of Durrow is still disputed. Other manuscripts were taken to the Continent, for example the illuminated Gospels of Saint Gall (Codex 51) with their twelve full-page miniatures and numerous ornamented initials. Splendid books like these would always have been rare, and one or the other might have perished or fallen into the hands of thieves or plunderers, who would covet the precious metal shrines in which such books were kept. The Annals of Ulster record a theft of the Book of Kells in the year 1007:

The big Gospel Book of Columcille, the outstanding relic of the West, was shamefully stolen from the western sacristy of the great stone church at Kells during the night because of its metal shrine. The book itself was rediscovered after two months and twenty nights; the gold had been removed, and the book was covered with turf.

A Gospel Book of similar splendour was seen by Giraldus Cambrensis at Kildare during the years 1185–8, and is described in his *Topography of Ireland:*

A BOOK MIRACULOUSLY WRITTEN

Among all the miracles of Kildare nothing seems to me more miraculous than that wonderful book which they say was written at the dictation of an angel during the lifetime of the virgin (St.Brigit). This book contains the four Gospels according to the concordance of St.Jerome, with almost as many drawings as pages, and all of them in marvellous colours. Here you can look upon the face of the divine majesty drawn in a miraculous way; here too upon the mystical representations of the Evangelists, now having six, now four, and now two, wings. Here you will see the eagle; there the calf. Here the face of a man; there that of a lion. And there are almost innumerable other drawings. If you look at them carelessly and casually and not too closely, you may judge them to be mere daubs rather than careful compositions. You will see nothing subtle where everything is subtle. But if you take the trouble to look very closely, and penetrate with your eyes to the secrets of the artistry, you will notice such intricacies, so delicate and subtle, so close together and well-knitted, so involved and bound together, and so fresh still in their colourings that you will not hesitate to declare that all these things must have been the result of the work, not of men, but of angels.

THE COMPOSITION OF THE BOOK

On the night before the day on which the scribe was to begin the book, an angel stood beside him in his sleep and showed him a drawing on a tablet which he carried in his hand, and said to him: "Do you think that you can make this drawing on the first page of the book that you are about to begin?" The scribe, not feeling that he was capable of an art so subtle, and trusting little in his knowledge of something almost unknown and very unusual, replied: "No." The angel said to him: "Tomorrow tell your lady, so that she may pour forth prayers for you to the Lord, that he may open both your bodily and mental eyes so as to see the more keenly and understand the more subtly, and may direct you in the guiding of your hand." All this was done, and on the following night the angel came again and held before him the same and many other drawings. By the help of the divine grace, the scribe, taking particular notice of them all, and faithfully committing them to his memory, was able to reproduce them exactly in the suitable places in the book. And so with the angel indicating the designs, Brigit praying, and the scribe imitating, that book was composed.

This story, which Giraldus must have been told at Kildare, resembles in some respects Bede's account of how Caedmon composed his Biblical epic. According to Giraldus, the manuscript would have been written in the fifth or the early sixth century. The description, however, clearly indicates that he must have seen a manuscript of the late seventh or eighth century. The "Book of Kildare" can have had as little to do with St.Brigit as the Book of Kells has to do with St.Columcille. Like many other treasures of Christian Ireland, the Book of Kildare has perished; we are grateful to Giraldus for his description of a lost masterpiece. The Book of Kildare must have been laid out on a similar scale to the Book of Kells. Some readers of Giraldus have even suggested that the manuscript which he described was actually the Book of Kells, and that he confused the two places. The legend of the origin of the Book of Kildare might be an indication of comparatively early origin, at a time when splendid illumination of this kind was something new. The Book of Kells, on the other hand, falls near the end of the golden age of Irish illumination and testifies to its full maturity. It is also influenced, if only slightly, by Carolingian art. We shall have more to say about it in the next chapter.

THE IRISH IN THE CAROLINGIAN EMPIRE

WE often speak of a Carolingian Renaissance. This historical term, though not entirely wrong, is to some extent misleading. Even the most superficial comparison of Carolingian culture with the Italian Renaissance of the fourteenth and fifteenth centuries reveals a fundamental difference, in scope as well as in attitude, between the reforms of learning inaugurated by Pipin and Charles on the one hand and the world of a Petrarch, Poggio, or Lorenzo Valla on the other. The so-called Carolingian Renaissance is not so much a revival of classical antiquity as a "renaissance" of late-antique Christianity, in particular of the age of the great Fathers of the Church. Speculative theology, which had been at a low ebb for two centuries, is resumed with a new vigour, and its problems, though posed in fresh terms, are largely those of the patristic age: the divinity and humanity of Christ, the Trinity, free will and predestination. Hand in hand with this revival of patristic theology goes a revival of ancient Christian poetry, from Iuvencus to Arator. A number of ninth-century manuscripts represent a Corpus of Christian Poets, to which is often added the *Consolation of Philosophy* by Boethius, a work written alternately in verse and prose. It was in the Carolingian schools that Boethius was given his place as the last classic of Latin literature. The study of these works, prose as well as poetry, would impress on the minds of enlightened readers the value of ancient secular literature as a source of information for their better understanding and also as a stylistic model for their own writings. Men who wished to write in the spirit and language of Christian antiquity would almost inevitably turn to the literature of pre-Christian Rome which had so evidently shaped the literary work of writers like Augustine or Prudentius. The basic school subjects of the *Artes*—the Trivium and Quadrivium—were no longer considered sufficient; they were supplemented by the study of Cicero and Virgil, and of Terence, Sallust, Horace, and other classical authors. In some degree this synthesis of Christian and classical elements had been achieved already by those men whom Charlemagne invited to his court from countries where a tradition of ancient culture was still in existence or had been revived before his time —Peter of Pisa, Theodulf of Orléans, Alcuin. At the turn of the seventh century, Northumbria had produced an author who was unequalled in his time as a theologian, historian, and encyclopedic writer—the Venerable Bede. In the Carolingian tradition of the Fathers Bede holds a place equal to that of the Christian classics, Ambrose, Jerome, Augustine, Cassiodorus, Gregory, and Isidore.

The reforms of Charlemagne as outlined in the Capitularia of the years 787 to 789 had strictly ecclesiastical objectives: a correct text of the Bible, the genuine Roman liturgy, and the restoration of a Christian way of life in world and cloister. Hence the Biblical text was thoroughly revised, standard texts of the Gregorian Sacramentary and of the Rule of St. Benedict were obtained from Italy. However, Charlemagne aimed higher. He wanted his clergy to read and to pray with the fullest possible understanding of their texts, and therefore to learn all that might help them to understand these texts better. Through its best representatives ecclesiastical education thus broadened—as it had done in the case of Cassiodorus—into a Christian humanism. But even the textual criticism of Lupus of Ferrière always remained subordinated to and directed towards his care for the preservation of the pure doctrine of Christianity.

Charlemagne went even one step further. He envisaged an educated laity as well as an educated clergy. His palace school, which was in the charge of Alcuin until, in 796, this great scholar became abbot of St. Martin at Tours, was open to the sons of the nobles whether they aimed at an ecclesiastical career or at a secular one. The Frankish nobility, however, was on the whole indifferent, and the

Emperor's efforts met with no lasting success. Until late in the Middle Ages Latin learning remained almost exclusively clerical.

In this cultural movement the Irish played an important, though not a decisive, role. Individually, some of them, for example Sedulius and Iohannes Scottus, are among the greatest scholars of that age. The inauguration of the new movement, however, owes little or nothing to the Irish. There certainly were Irish scholars at the court of Charlemagne. They were held in honour, but at the same time they were felt to be strangers, to be different not only from Spaniards and Lombards but also from an Anglo-Saxon such as Alcuin. Occasionally they met with hostility. A man of the Old World like the Spaniard Theodulf would class them as upstarts who did not know how to carry their learning lightly. The Irish rose to importance again under Charlemagne's successors, under his son Louis the Pious and in particular under his grandson Charles the Bald, who was a pupil of the learned Walahfrid Strabo. In the early Carolingian period their influence is not so manifest. That it existed is proved by the Irish elements of Alcuin's education at York, which date from Egbert's time. The story about the origins of the new learning which is read at the beginning of the *Gesta Karoli Magni*—a Saint Gall product of the 880's, of disputed authorship—is, however, entirely legendary:

When the all-powerful Lord, who makes kings and deposes them and who establishes the sequence of empires and ages, had broken the feet of iron and clay of His wonderful statue among the Romans, He set up the head of a statue not less wonderful among the Franks in the person of the noble Charles. As soon as he had become sole monarch in the West—at a time when learned studies almost everywhere had fallen into almost complete oblivion—it so happened that two Scots from Ireland, men unrivalled in the knowledge of profane and sacred writings, landed on the coast of Gaul in the company of British merchants. Crowds gathered in order to purchase goods. The two Irishmen, having no wares to offer, kept on shouting: "If anybody desires wisdom, let him come to us and acquire it, for we have it for sale." This they said in order to attract people who evidently had come merely for making purchases and to suggest to them that among other things they should also acquire wisdom; perhaps—as will be confirmed by the continuation of this story—they also wished to cause surprise and gain admiration. They continued to advertise their wares until those people, partly because of the strangeness of the incident, partly because they thought these men were mad, reported to King Charles what had happened. The king, who loved and desired wisdom, called them to his presence immediately and asked them whether they really possessed wisdom as they asserted. They replied: "We do possess it, and in the name of the Lord we are willing to impart it to all those who desire it in the right spirit." When the king asked what they demanded for themselves, they said: "Nothing more than a place suitable for the teaching of receptive minds and those things which are needed on man's pilgrimage through life—food and clothing." This answer greatly pleased the king. He kept the two scholars at his court for some time. But when he had to go to war, he told the one, Clemens by name, to stay in Gaul and made him educator of a large number of boys, of high, medium, and low station; he provided them with everything they needed, and assigned them suitable living quarters. The other (Albinus, according to some manuscripts) was sent by the king to Italy. He took up residence in the monastery of St. Augustine near the city of Ticinum, where all those who wished to learn from him assembled.

Here, as in other literature of the later ninth century, the great achievements of Irish scholars in the mid-century are projected back into the beginnings of the Carolingian revival.

As a historical phenomenon this flocking of Irish scholars to the courts and episcopal sees of Carolingian Gaul differs essentially from the Irish mission of the seventh and early eighth centuries. The Irish come no longer as preachers of the Gospel or as "exiles for the sake of Christ". An exception FINTAN to the rule is St. Fintan, who on his return from a pilgrimage to Rome stayed as an anchorite on the island of Rheinau near Schaffhausen, and later as an *inclusus* in the monastery of Honau, where he died in or about 878. The majority of Irishmen who crossed the sea to France were attracted by the new cultural centres and wished to make contact with the revival of learning on the Continent. Virgil's Aethicus Ister had commented sadly on the decline of learning in the Ireland of his time:

"He also went to Ireland and stayed among the Irish for some time in order to study their books. He called their monks and scholars eccentric, and said they were workers without skill and teachers without learning. He writes with scorn: 'To go to the end of the world and visit Ireland is great toil without profit. One exposes oneself to all sorts of horrors and gets nothing in return. The peasants do not know their work and the people have no teachers.'"

It seems that even at the end of the eighth century the intellectual élite of Ireland had made their way to Aix-la-Chapelle.

The attraction which intellectual life on the Continent began to have for Irish scholars coincided with a desperate situation at home which would have tended to drive them away. In the year 795 the Norsemen (mainly Norwegians, later also Danes) had unexpectedly attacked Lambay Island in the Bay of Dublin, and this attack opened a long series of raids during which one after the other of Ireland's ancient churches and monasteries fell a prey to the northern pirates. They did not limit their attacks to the coast and the off-shore islands, but sailed up the estuaries of rivers as far as these were navigable and thus penetrated deeply into the country. Things became even worse when in about 830 the Viking prince Turgesius made Dublin his permanent headquarters. Other fortified settlements of the Vikings followed: Wexford, Waterford, Limerick. They were all bases of operations, from which the surrounding countryside was systematically plundered. Churches and monasteries, which were built mostly of timber or other combustible material, went up in flames. Reliquaries, metal shrines for books, and other articles of commercial value were looted. The books, which meant nothing to the plunderers, were left to their fate or thrown into the water. Monks and clerics were lucky if they saved their lives, and possibly succeeded in rescuing one or the other of their sacred treasures, a relic or a precious manuscript. The loot was taken home by the raiders. Some of it, for example chalices or reliquaries, could be turned immediately to profane use. An Irish reliquary, which served as jewel box for a Norwegian lady, may still be seen in the Museum at Copenhagen. Other articles were taken apart, and the pieces used as ornaments on various objects. Like most non-Christian nations, the Norsemen had the custom of burying with their dead some of their most treasured possessions, and thus the tombs of Scandinavia have yielded large finds of Irish *objets d'art*, both sacred and profane, of the eighth and ninth centuries. The victory of the Irish on Lough Foyle (867) and soon afterwards their victory on land near Drogheda put an end to Viking power in the northern part of the island. In the south their rule continued for another century and was broken only after the Irish seized and destroyed the wealthy town of Limerick in 967. Brian Boru's victory at Clontarf in 1014 at last forced the Norsemen to abandon Ireland for good.

In such circumstances monasticism, which during the seventh and eighth centuries had already lapsed so badly into worldliness that it called for the reform of the Culdees, was bound to sink much lower still. Not even the Viking terror, however, was able to destroy it completely. It survived in places, and with it survived some tradition of monastic learning. Without such a continued tradition, however rare it may have become, it would be inexplicable how Irish poets and scholars who appear in mid-ninth-century France were able to impress their contemporaries by an erudition that was as wide as it was profound. Another witness to the religious spirit of Ireland under the Vikings is the considerable number of Irish pilgrims visiting Rome, who by that time had at their disposal a widespread net of hospices all along their route. The "wandering Irish" *(Scotti peregrini)* moved not only in one direction; contacts were mutual, it was a matter of give and take. There was even something like a half-way house: the court of Gwynned in North Wales, where, in the same way as under the

Carolingians in France and under Alfred the Great in Wessex, a culture had come to maturity which was partly ecclesiastical and Latin, partly national.

ALCUIN   The centre of intellectual life at the court of Charlemagne was an Anglo-Saxon, Alcuin. As a result of his meeting with the king at Parma in 781 he had come to France first as a visitor, then, in 793, he settled there permanently. He was first and foremost a theologian, and as such intervened in the questions of adoptianism and of the cult of images. At the same time Alcuin is an excellent example of the effect which the humanistic element in the writings of the Fathers could have. Alcuin was intimately acquainted with a fair amount of ancient literature, and what is more, he loved it, even though in his more scrupulous moments he felt a sense of guilt about the pleasure it gave him. When writing on the *Artes*, he expounded them in lively dialogue, which may be taken as a symptom of personal involvement. Some of his poems are spontaneous expressions of personal experience (most strikingly so the *Versus de Cuculo*, written for an unfaithful disciple) and thus rise above the purely formal scholastic versification of his time. This attitude of mind is well shown in the name Flaccus, which Alcuin had chosen as a member of Charlemagne's Academy.

That Alcuin had connexions with Ireland is proved by several letters in his correspondence. These connexions should be neither over-rated nor under-rated. There is no reason for believing that Alcuin had studied in Ireland or that he had ever been there. The *magister* Colcu to whom one of his letters is addressed need not be identical with Colcu úa Duinechda, who, according to the Annals of the Four Masters, was a monk of Clonmacnoise and died in 796; far more probably Alcuin's correspondent was an Irish teacher at York. Neither is Alcuin's presence in Ireland proved by his interest in the Northumbrian monastery of Mayo. Bishop Aldwulf of Mayo was present at an English synod under the presidency of the papal legate George of Ostia in 786, where Alcuin might easily have met him. Alcuin's "son" (that is, pupil) Joseph, whom he specifies as a compatriot of Colcu, had probably gone to York for his studies and had both Colcu and Alcuin as his teachers. This Joseph is probably the author of several acrostic religious poems dedicated to Charlemagne. Alcuin bears witness not so much to direct Irish-Frankish relations as to the continued influence of the Irish in Northumbria. He was also an intermediary between these two cultures. In the course of his revision of the Gregorian Sacramentary he preserved the best of the Gallican liturgy and incorporated it in the Roman Missal, and he introduced into the Frankish liturgy Irish-Northumbrian customs such as the chanting of the Creed at Mass and the celebration of the feast of All Saints. It has often been said that Alcuin played a decisive part in the creation of Caroline minuscule, the new calligraphic book hand which is the prototype of our Roman alphabet; this, however, is as far from being certain as is the dependence of Carolingian minuscule on the insular script.

CLEMENS   One of the first heads of the palace school, perhaps Alcuin's immediate successor, was the Irishman Clemens, who has already been mentioned in a different context. A Latin grammar ascribed to him is valuable because it contains extracts from earlier works which are lost. To what extent the knowledge of these authors shown by Clemens (and generally the knowledge of ancient authors on the part of Irishmen on the Continent) reflects the scholastic standards of the Irish at home is an open question. Even if the attribution of this work to Clemens is not too well founded, it certainly is the work of an Irish scholar in the Frankish kingdom.

DUNGAL   Dungal, a monk of Saint-Denis, was a poet as well as a scholar. At the request of the Emperor Charles this versatile Irishman wrote a treatise on the eclipse of the sun in 810, and a defence of the cult of saints and their images against the iconoclast Claudius of Turin in 827. He is probably the same Dungal who wrote several Latin poems, among them the panegyric of *Hibernicus Exul* on Charles's victory over Thassilo, Duke of Bavaria. There is some reason for identifying him also with Dungal of Pavia, whom Lothar in 825 entrusted with the direction of learned studies and education in Northern Italy.

Little is known about Dicuil, author of verses *De Grammatica*, of an astronomical treatise, and of a work on geography. The little that we know about him is derived from his own writings. When, in 814, he began to write on astronomy, he was already well established in the court circle. The treatise was finished in 816 and was dedicated to Charlemagne's successor, Louis the Pious. At that time Dicuil might have been the head of the palace school. The date of the geographical work can be given as 825. In this work Dicuil writes about the presence of Irish hermits on the north-western islands as an eye-witness and reports their expulsion by the Norsemen. He had probably been a monk in Ireland before he came to France, perhaps as a refugee from the Vikings. The Suibne whom he mentions as his master could easily be Abbot Suibne of Iona, who died in 772. It is arguable that the plundering of Iona by the Norsemen in 806 was the immediate cause of Dicuil's exile.

The work on astronomy is not remarkable from the scientific point of view. As a piece of literature it has some interest because its prose is interspersed with verse, which is rhythmical and not metrical on the ancient model. Dicuil's geographical treatise, on the other hand, the *Liber de Mensura Orbis Terrae*, is not only the best book on geography during the early Middle Ages but is also evidence of the survival of important geographical literature of classical Rome. One of Dicuil's sources was a survey *(Mensuratio* or *Divisio Orbis Terrae)* which the Emperor Theodosius II had ordered in 435; this survey, which was based on the earlier survey of Augustus and Agrippa, was present in the library of Charlemagne. Dicuil was not original, and did not aim at originality, but he was surprisingly well read in the geographical literature of the Romans from Pliny the Elder down to Isidore. In the section on north-western Europe, which was little known in antiquity, he adds some details from his own observation. There we read as follows:

In the sea to the north-west of Spain, so we read, there are no islands. Around our own island, Ireland, there are islands, but some of them are small and some tiny. In the vicinity of Britain there are many islands, some small, some large, some of medium size; some of these are situated in the south and west, but the majority are in the north-west and north. In some of these I have lived, others I have visited, others I have seen, and about others I have merely read....

Speaking of Britain, Julius Solinus in his Collectanea says (about Thule, i.e. Iceland): "Thule lies at the end of the world. At the time of the summer solstice, when the sun passes through the sign of Cancer, there is no night in that island; at the time of the winter solstice, there is no day there."

It is now thirty years since clerics, who had stayed in that island from the first of February to the first of August, reported to me that not only on the day of the summer solstice but also on the days immediately before and after that date the sun, when it sets in the evening, is just barely hidden as behind a low hill. In this short time during which the sun hides it naturally does not get dark, and one can do whatever one wishes, even pick the lice from one's shirt, just as well as if the sun were visible. And if those clerics had stood on top of a mountain on that island, they might even have seen the sun all the time. At the moment which divides that short time evenly (that is, when the sun is at its lowest point) it is midnight on the equator. Similarly, I believe, on the day of the winter solstice and for some days before and after it one can see in Thule something like dawn just for a short time when it is mid-day on the equator. Those writers who have asserted that the sea around Thule freezes in winter, and that Thule has one continuous day from the spring equinox to the autumn equinox, and one continous night from the autumn equinox to the spring equinox, either lie or are in error. The sailors whom I have mentioned landed on the island about the time when, according to the course of nature, the lowest temperature was to be expected, and during their stay there was regular alternation of day and night, except at the time of the solstice. One day's journey farther north, however, they did find the sea frozen.

In the sea to the north of Britain there are also many other islands, which can be reached from the islands off the northern shore in two days and nights, if one takes a direct course, with sails hoisted and a good wind. A pious priest told me that he made the journey to one of these islands in two summer days and one night between them in a small boat with only two seats. Some of these islands are small, and almost all of them are separated from one another only by narrow straits. For a period of about a hundred years hermits from our island used to go to these islands and to live there. Now, after cruel attacks by the northern pirates, no anchorites are left there, and these islands are as unhabited as they had been since the beginning of time, except for innumerable sheep and all kinds of sea-birds. These islands I have not found mentioned in any books of the ancients.

DONATUS OF FIESOLE Carolingian France can also claim the one and only hagiographical epic composed by an Irishman. It is a Life of St. Brigit, written in well constructed Latin hexameters and in fluent and vivid language. In one of the prologues the author gives his name as Bishop Donatus. This is in all probability the Irishman Donatus who was bishop of Fiesole from 826 to 877. Mario Esposito is probably right in his conjecture that Donatus wrote not only the prologue but the entire work. With all her wealth of hagiographical legend, Ireland has produced nothing to match this poem. The only other Life of an Irish saint in Latin verse, as far as we know, is a *Vita* of St. Senan in rhyming dimeters; it belongs to an entirely different literary tradition. The poem of Donatus must be studied against the background of such ninth-century works as the metrical *Vita* of St. Gall and the hagiographical epics of Heiric of Auxerre and Milo of Saint-Amand.

Among the many Irish scholars who in those days trod the roads of Europe two stand out by the wide range of their interests, their mastery of the Latin language, and a certain knowledge of Greek, but above all by their genius. They are known to us as Sedulius Scottus and Iohannes Scottus.

SEDULIUS SCOTTUS Sedulius arrived in France in about 848. He and his companions, wandering scholars like himself, found a patron in Bishop Hartgar of Liège. One of the poems of Sedulius (II. 3) apparently recalls their first meeting:

Dread-visaged Boreas blows rimy blasts and we
shrink back in terror from sudden darts and threats;
trembles the very land, white-stricken with great fear,
and sea cries out and the hard rocks moan;
now menaces he the spaces of the air
with dread-arousing cries and thundering roar;
sky's milky fleece is covered with glowering cloud
and earth is pallid in a snow-white gown;
and suddenly the woodland sheds its hair
and stout oak starts trembling like a reed;
the sun, once wont to shine resplendently,
withholds his rays, now hides his very face;
ah woe! tumultuous Boreas has us all undone,
we learned teachers, yes, and pious priests,
for eagle Northwind has no regard of state
and mangles even us with cruel beak.

Then, Hartgar, powerful prelate, raise the weak,
cherish the learned Irish with gentle heart,

Ornamented initials from the Grammar of Priscian at St. Gall.

so, blessed, in heaven's high temples may you walk,
Celestial Jerusalem and enduring Zion.

Great prelate! His mercy and his quiet mind
conquered the blasts and tamed old Boreas' pride;
kindly took he the weary in, and bountiful
snatched three scholars from the howling winds,
clothing us and honouring all three
so we became that gentle shepherd's sheep.

Hartgar was pleased with the learning, the wit, and the poetic talent of Sedulius and his friends. They stayed at Liège, and it would seem that in course of time they became the nucleus of a small colony of Irish scholars. The bishop took it upon himself to look after the needs of his (not too ascetical) protégés, and from time to time Sedulius sent him a gentle reminder in the form of a poem like this one (II. 49):

The crops are green and fields are all in flower,
budding the vine—the year now has its hour;
gay-painted songbirds fill the air with glee,
there's smile on land and sky and laughs the sea.

Of mirth-provoking sap I too have need,
some beer, or Bacchus' gift, or perhaps some mead;
and then there's meat, produce of earth and sky,
and I have none, but ask the reason why.

Now, Muse, I write and sing, am Orpheus reborn,
but too have needs, the ox that treads the corn;
your champion I, with wisdom's arms I fight:
Off Muse to the bishop, acquaint him with my plight.

We do not know how long before his arrival in France Sedulius had left Ireland. It seems that he had spent some time at the court of King Rhodri Mawr of Gwynned. A poem of thanksgiving for a victory of the Irish over the Vikings possibly dates from his Welsh or Irish days (II. 45):

Rejoice ye heavens, sea and all the land;
ye people too who wax in Christ,
see the great deeds of the Lord, the Father,
*   thundering Godhead.*

Most worthy of praises, sole author of good,
great in great deeds, blessed creator,
holding firmament's sceptre and with nod of the brow
*   all things disposing.*

World's holy ruler, its hope and salvation,
levelling mountain, raising the valley,
crushing the wicked, crowning the humble,
    omnipotent power.

Christ the True Light He causes to shine
on faithful hearts, on mirror of the mind,
cherishing them with constancy,
    sustaining creator.

Ye rich and poor, ye high and humble,
clerics too, His tonsured order,
be ye young or old, mankind or women,
    praise Him ye all.

The stout strong arm of a powerful father
with sudden fury has now prostrated
foes of the faithful, the rebel Northman;
    glory to the Father.

The fight is joined on open plain
and weapons glitter in the limpid air
and warrior cry might seem to shake
    the scaffolding of sky.

Opposing lines unleash their spearshafts,
unhappy Northman counts his losses,
a mighty army aims and places
    its showers of iron.

Those who have thirsted down through the years
are quaffing the blood of a savage oppressor
and finding sweet savour in nourishing breast
    on the slaughter of men.

Those who set snares stand there ensnared,
topples a tower reaching to the sky;
A hostile horde, swelling with pride,
    Christ has undone them.

There is there laid low a stout strong people,
a cursed mass has now been crumbled,
an evil issue death's maw has swallowed;
    be praised, O Christ.

Ornaments from the Book of Kells.

122

Now can be reckoned a mighty slaughter:
count not unknown, count not the menials,
on that dread field lay bloody there
three times ten thousand.

The judge is just, lord of the world,
Christ the true glory of Christian people,
magnificent ruler, vanquishing evil
in high jurisdiction.

Great tower is He, and shield of salvation,
undoing in battle the strength of the giants,
Whose name is high above all names
and ever blessed.

A faithful people has that great avenger
who unleashed the sea in swelling torrents
on proud Egyptian, overwhelming all,
chariots, horsemen.

Christ wearing purple now reigns over
what high Begetter first created,
blessed scion of the House of David
and our glory.

He to Whom we offer incense,
Whom we name in act of prayer,
King of stars Whom we intone
on pipe of praise.

Now cry ye glory and cry Hosanna,
now sing of Father, begotten Christ
and Holy Spirit; sky, earth and water
praise Him ye all.

Many of Sedulius's poems are court poetry. He might be described as a bard in Latin dress. The Emperor Lothar and King Charles the Bald, who by the treaty of Verdun (843) had obtained the western kingdom, must soon have become aware of this powerful poet. Sedulius is at his most human, however, when he writes for Hartgar. Among these poems is the most original one that he ever wrote (II. 41), a mock-necrology on a ram in the bishop's herd, which had been torn to pieces by a hound, and which, as Sedulius intimates, had been set aside as a gift for Hartgar's Irish friend. Since the days of Hellenistic literature mourning for animals had been fashionable as a theme of poetry. Sedulius's poem, however, surpasses in sophistication all its predecessors. The ram had been stolen, but the thief escaped, and the hounds who had chased him attacked in their fury the animal which he had left behind. The snow-white ram is described in all its beauty, a match even for Aries in the sky. By way of contrast, the thief is given all the attributes of wickedness. The fight of the ram with the hounds is told in the parodistical style of the animal-epic, including elaborate speeches on either side. When at last the ram is defeated, the poet boldly compares him to the Lamb of God: he, too, has saved a thief's soul by his vicarious death and thus given the evil-doer time for repentance! Yet the pious poet speaks with his tongue in his cheek. Here are some lines, by way of illustration, where, in mock-heroic fashion, he praises the dead ram's virtues:

> *Wherein his guilt—so simple, straight and true?*
> *Bacchus he shunned, sherbet avoided too;*
> *not him did liquor from narrow path entice,*
> *nor meal with king, or lesser lord, his vice;*
> *his solemn feast was grazing on the grass,*
> *his sweetest drink from brink of limpid Maas,*
> *nor did he plead that he be vested in*
> *purple or red—felt happy with a skin;*
> *and never did he ride astride a horse*
> *but steady on his legs he plied a course,*
> *lied not, nor idle word did ever say,*
> *but utterance of depth—just "baa" and "beh".*

However, at the bottom of so much mourning there is the poet's deep regret that the fine specimen of a ram, whose frugality he, all too fond of food and drink, has ironically exalted, was not to grace his table, and he ends his necrology with these moving words:

> *Adieu good chief of gleaming herd—alas*
> *I see you not a-feeding on my grass.*
> *Ah! Were you there a hot bath I had planned*
> *(only to please the guest you understand!)*
> *and self would minister with devoted breast*
> *to head and horn and hoof and all the rest.*
> *You have I loved, and love your widow too,*
> *mother I love, and brothers all—Adieu.*

Sedulius has, with some justification, been claimed as the ancestor of goliardic poetry. At the same time he was a scholar of universal interests. We still possess a Greek (and partly Graeco-Latin) psalter in his hand; other bilingual Biblical texts, among them a copy of the Gospels and one of the Pauline Epistles, have been attributed to his circle on less secure grounds. Sedulius also wrote commentaries on some Biblical books. His commentary on St. Paul makes use, among other sources, of the commentary by Pelagius. From Sedulius's circle also came manuscripts of Priscian with Irish glosses, now at Leiden and Saint Gall, and he himself commented on a grammatical work. Codex Bernensis 363 gives some idea of Sedulius's literary equipment: there we find extracts from grammatical, rhetorical, and dialectical works, from glosses on Virgil, from the *Metamorphoses* of Ovid, and above all a considerable portion of the poems of Horace, a poet whom Sedulius not only imitated in matters of form, but in whom he recognized a kindred spirit. Another collection of extracts, preserved only in a late copy, now in the library of the Ancient Hospital of Cues on the Moselle, is related to Sedulius's work *On*

Christian Rulers. This work, written alternately in prose and verse in imitation of the *Consolatio* of Boethius, has a place among the earliest "Mirrors of Princes".

Sedulius always bore his learning lightly, and found a way of reconciling his sincere piety with his enjoyment of the good things of this life. He knew that he was no saint of the type of Irish ascetics, but he was never unduly troubled by his human weaknesses. Sinner that he is, he commends himself to the grace of God and to the Virgin Mary at the end of a short poem in which he sketches his own portrait in a Horatian vein (II. 74):

I read and write and teach, philosophy peruse,
I eat and freely drink, with rhymes invoke the muse,
I call on heaven's throne both night and day,
snoring I sleep, or stay awake and pray.

And sin and fault inform the life I plan:
Ah! Christ and Mary pity this miserable man.

IOHANNES
SCOTTUS

About the same time as Sedulius Scottus at Liège, John Scottus was active at Laon. Like Sedulius Scottus, John Scottus was the centre of a circle of Irish scholars. A member of this circle, the Irishman Martinus, is known as the scribe of a Graeco-Latin manuscript (Laon 444), which gives a good idea of the nature and extent of Greek studies among this Irish colony. They covered elementary grammar, Graeco-Latin glossaries, and a limited knowledge of the Greek text of the Bible; occasionally somebody made a feeble attempt at writing Greek verse. According to Dom Cappuyns, Laon was at that time the seat of the palace school, in which Charles the Bald took a personal interest. John, who apparently had coined for himself the high-sounding epithet "scion of Ireland" (Eriugena), was its most prominent teacher.

About the life of John Eriugena we know very little. He is first heard of as an opponent of Gottschalk, who had been made a monk against his will, and turned into a brooding thinker and finally a heretic. His radical doctrine on predestination had been condemned by the Council of Mainz in 848 and he himself had been severely punished. The problem, however, which he had raised was much discussed, and a number of orthodox theologians felt called upon to write in defence of free will. The chief champion of orthodoxy was Bishop Hincmar of Reims. The bishop invited John to join the ranks of Gottschalk's critics. John must have already had a reputation for learning, and not only as a teacher of the *Artes* (in which capacity he had written a commentary on Martianus Capella); otherwise he, a layman for all that we know, would hardly have been called upon to pronounce on a fundamental problem of theology. The treatise *On Predestination*, which in response to Bishop Hincmar's wish he produced in 851, rather puzzled his patrons, Hincmar and his suffragan Pardulf of Laon. The dialectical method which John applied to that theological question was in his time something unheard of. What was worse, his refutation of Gottschalk's doctrine took the line of denying the possibility of predestination on the grounds of the Neoplatonic theory that evil had no real existence. We cannot name with certainty John's source for this doctrine; he probably derived it from the Neoplatonic elements in the works of St. Augustine and from some Greek theologians whose works were available in Latin translations. The critic of Gottschalk must have shocked the orthodox no less than the criticized, and was in his turn attacked by Prudentius of Troyes and Florus of Lyons. His book was even officially condemned at two French synods. One would expect that John's relations with Hincmar received a severe blow, but of this there is no proof. The alleged proof, a satirical epitaph on the (still living) Hincmar (d. 882), is now considered spurious.

If there was any estrangement at all, it cannot have lasted long. Only a few years later Charles the Bald entrusted John with a Latin translation of the Greek writings of the so-called Areopagite. These writings—four treatises and ten letters—purported to be the work of Denis (Dionysius) the Areopagite, the convert of the apostle Paul after his preaching at Athens (Acts 17.34). In reality they were written by an unknown Christian Neoplatonist of the late fifth century. The teaching of the Pseudo-Areopagite is a mystical theology with a certain pantheistic trend. The Church at first received these writings with considerable reserve, but in course of time the opinion that their author was really the convert of St. Paul gained the upper hand, and by the seventh century they were generally regarded as genuine. A copy of the Greek text is said to have been given to Pipin by Pope Paul I in 757. We know for certain that a copy of the Greek Dionysius was presented to Louis the Pious by the Byzantine Emperor Michael II in 827. Louis passed this present on to his court chaplain and spiritual adviser, Abbot Hilduin of Saint-Denis near Paris, and demanded of him a Latin translation, which was actually made during the years 831–835. For France these writings had a certain topical interest because the Areopagite, the alleged author of those texts, had become identified with the patron saint of Saint-Denis, a Bishop Dionysius, who at some unknown date had suffered martyrdom near Paris with two companions. Hilduin's translation left much to be desired, and Charles was anxious to avail himself of John's knowledge of Greek, which was exceptional for his time, in order to get a better translation. John based his translation on that of Hilduin, but changed it in many places—and not always for the better. In his preface he apologizes to the king for any shortcomings, saying that he is only a beginner in Greek studies. This may largely be a conventional show of modesty, but it probably contains a grain of truth. The Greek which John had learnt at home hardly went beyond the teaching attested by Codex 444 of Laon. Gradually, however, being unusually gifted in languages as well as in philosophical speculation, he rose to his task. Later he translated successfully works of Maximus Confessor and other Greek theologians. Even his translation of Pseudo-Dionysius is, by and large, both faithful and intelligent. This translation was probably made between the years 860 and 862. Again, John seems to have come in for some criticism—this time concerning the fidelity and competence of his translation. On the authenticity of a letter addressed to Charles the Bald by Pope Nicholas I, in which the Pope demands a copy of the work for examination, opinions are divided. It is a fact, however, that the papal librarian, Anastasius, revised John's translation, annotated it with glosses taken from a Greek commentary, and returned this copy together with a letter to the king. The revision of the papal librarian does not seem to have been very thorough. His criticism is almost entirely confined to a regret that John, in an endeavour to be as faithful to the original as possible, had not gone far enough towards making the obscurities of the text intelligible. John himself may have felt the same; in later years he began to write a commentary on his translation.

In the Christian Neoplatonism of the "Areopagite", whose teaching was accepted without suspicion, John could not help seeing a confirmation and justification of his own theological ideas. Thus in the middle of the 860's, under the influence of Pseudo-Dionysius, he wrote a large work in five books in which he developed an elaborate theological system. Its basic concept is the emanation from God of all that is created, and the eventual return of all creatures to their origin. The title of the work was originally *On the Division of Nature (De Divisione Naturae)*, but this was later changed to *On the Natures (Periphyseon)*. Of this change of title, and of successive revisions to which this work was subjected by its author we have direct evidence in a number of manuscripts which date from the author's time and which, apparently, were written under his eye and, in all probability, annotated by his own hand. John dedicated his work to his friend Wulfad, who later (866) was made bishop of Bourges. A summary of John's system is best given in his own words, towards the end of the fifth book:

We have made a fourfold division of all nature, a term by which we understand God and His creation. Firstly we contemplate and distinguish nature that creates and is not created; secondly nature that is created and creates; thirdly nature that is created and does not create; and lastly nature that neither is created nor creates. The first and fourth kind can be predicated only of God. This is not to say that God's nature, which is simple and more-than-simple, admits of division, but merely that it permits contemplation under two aspects. For when I contemplate the origin and ultimate cause of all things, then my mind is impressed by the truth that the divine essence or substance, goodness, power, wisdom, and whatever else is predicated of God, is not created by anything, because there is nothing beyond and above divine nature, but everything that is or is not is created by it, through it, in it, and towards it. If, however, I contemplate the same essence as the final goal of all things, and my mind dwells on its being the ultimate limit beyond which nothing can go, for which everything strives and where all natural movement comes to rest, then I realize that it is neither created nor does it create. Nature cannot be created out of anything else, because it is of itself. Neither does it create anything, for seeing that everything that is produced by it in the way of intellectual or sensibly perceptible generation must return into it in a re-generation which is wondrous beyond words and everything will be at rest in it because nothing further proceeds from it by new generation, one is entitled to say that it creates nothing. What, I ask, should it create when it will be everything in everything and nothing will be manifest in it but itself? As regards the two kinds between the extremes, enough has been said about them in the preceding pages. They are clear to anyone who cares to investigate them. The one is seen in the first causes, the other in the effects of these causes. The one that consists in the causes is created by the only-begotten Son of God, in whom and through whom all has been created. This nature, in turn, creates everything that emanates from it, that is to say, all its effects, whether they are purely intelligible or perceptible to the senses. The other kind, which consists in the effects of the (first) causes, is created by its own causes but creates nothing, because there is nothing lower in the nature of things. Therefore it consists mainly in those things which can be perceived by the senses.

This need not exclude the possibility that angels or human beings, whether they are good or evil, should often have created something in this world that was new and unknown to the use of man. These beings do not create anything, but merely form something out of the material creation which has been created by God out of its causes, it being their effect. If men are good, they do this in obedience to the divine laws and commandments; if they are bad, they act under the influence and illusion of the devil's fraudulent cunning. All the same, everything is ordained by the providence of God so that there is no evil as a substance in the nature of things—nothing that could disturb the communion and, as it were, the social order of all things.

Having contemplated the four aspects of all nature in its four kinds—two of which, being origin and end, are found in the divine nature, two others, being causes and effects, belong to created nature—we have felt justified in adding some theories concerning the return of the effects to their causes, that is to say, to their essential causes. This return is understood in a threefold manner: The first one, in a general way, is seen in the transformation of all sensible creation within this world, that is, of all bodies, whether they are actually perceived by the senses or escape sense perception because of their being utterly minute; as a result, not a single body remains in the fabric of corporeal nature, neither a body that is moved, secretly or manifestly, only by the motion of life nor one that has an irrational soul and bodily senses. They all return, through life, to their hidden causes, for nothing can be annihilated in anything that from the cause of all things as its substance has received substantial existence. The second form of contemplation is appropriate to the general return of all human nature saved by Christ to its original state of creation, to the dignity of the image of God, and as it were to Paradise, through the merit of the One, whose blood has been shed for the common salvation of all mankind. Thus no human being will be deprived of those natural goods in whose possession that being has been created, no matter whether in this life he was good or wicked. In this way the indescribable and incomprehensible effusion of divine goodness and mercy over all human nature will be made manifest, if in no human being will that which comes from the supreme good be punished. The third form of contemplation applies to those who shall rise not only to the natural excellency of their substance, but by an overflow of divine grace which is given by Christ and in Christ to His elect transcend their own essence beyond all laws and limits of nature and shall enter into God Himself and become one in Him and with Him. In their return to their origin we can, so to say, discern seven steps. The first is the transformation of the physical body into the motion of life. The second is the transformation of vital motion into sense perception. The third is the transformation of sense perception into reason. Then follows the transformation of reason into mind, and this is the end and goal of all rational creation. After this integration of the five parts, if I may say so,

128

of our nature, namely body, vital motion, sense perception, reason, and mind, which are then no longer five, but only one, because the lower one is always resolved in the higher one (not in such a way that they are no longer, but in such a way that they all are one), there follow the other three steps of the ascent. One of these is the transition of mind to a knowledge of all things that are less than God. The second is the transition of knowledge to wisdom, that is, an intimate contemplation of truth as far as this is possible for a creature. The third and highest is the supernatural submersion of the purest minds into God Himself, into the darkness, as it were, of the incomprehensible and inaccessible light, in which are hidden the causes of all things; and then the night will shine like the day, that is to say, the most intimate of the divine mysteries will be revealed in an indescribable manner to those blessed and illumined minds. Then the perfection of the number Eight, a supernatural cube, so to speak, will be established for ever, having been foreshadowed by the title of the sixth psalm: "Psalm of David, for the eighth day". For the resurrection of Our Lord also took place on the eighth day, in order to intimate mystically that blessed life which after the sevenfold rotation of the seven days of this life will follow upon the end of the world. Similarly, as we have said, human nature returns to its origin by an eightfold ascent: a fivefold one within the limits of its own nature, and a threefold one, transcending its nature and essence, within God Himself. When the Fiveness of created nature has been united to the Threeness of the creator, then there is nothing manifest at any step but God alone, similarly as in the purest air only the light shines.

This, then, is the subject of this work in five books. If anybody finds that in it we have written anything novel or unnecessary, may he attribute this to our lack of discipline and prudence and, in the humility of his pious heart, forgive a human mind which is still burdened by his house of flesh. For in our life here on earth, which is obscured by mists, no human endeavour can, I think, be perfect or free from all error. The just also, who still live in the flesh, are so called not because they are really just, but because they desire to be just and strive for perfect justice in the future they are so called by virtue of their heart's desire.... If, however, a reader finds to his delight anything that is profitable, anything that aids his edification in the Catholic faith, then let him attribute this to God alone, who alone can disperse the cloud of darkness and lead those who seek Him to Himself, free from all illusion and all error.... Without prejudice to those who may take kindly to this our common work, reading it with limpid purity of mind, or, perhaps, turn away from it in ill-will and in their bias condemn it even before they have found out what it is about and how the subject is treated, I offer this work first of all to God..., then to you, my beloved brother in Christ and fellow-searcher for truth, Wulfad, for examination and correction. You have given me the courage to embark on it, and it is your merit if I have completed it as best I could.... Let everyone be guided by his own spirit until the coming of that light which changes the light of the false philosophers to darkness and the darkness of the true knowledge-seekers to light.

A platonizing theologian, Eriugena builds up a comprehensive theory of nature with the help of Boethian dialectics. The elements are all borrowed: from Pseudo-Dionysius, Boethius, Augustine, and in particular from such Greek theologians as Epiphanius, Gregory of Nyssa, and Maximus, from whom he quotes passages in his own translation. The synthesis, however, is entirely his. It is the first of its kind, and for a long time it remained the only one. That Eriugena's theology is pantheistic has as often been asserted as it has been denied. He himself, like all medieval authors, was most anxious to avoid unorthodoxy; even as a scholar he would have considered heretical opinions to be unscientific. He saw no contradiction between his theological system and the teaching of the Church, since, as he and his contemporaries believed, he had on his side the authority of a disciple of the apostle Paul. When the work first appeared it probably aroused more bewilderment than opposition. Its subject was difficult and unfamiliar, the treatment abstract, the whole work too far removed from the theological thought of the times. It was nevertheless copied and excerpted more than once during the ninth century, and occasionally even later—as late, in fact, as the thirteenth century. However, when Amaury of Bène and his circle taught an outspoken pantheism and claimed Eriugena as their authority, his work was

Opposite:
High Cross of Abbot
Muiredach at
Monasterboice,
Co. Louth.

131

condemned—first at a synod of Paris in 1210, then finally by Pope Honorius in 1225. The translation of Pseudo-Dionysius, which was the basis of John's system, enjoyed as much authority as ever, and was even retranslated several times during the late Middle Ages.

Marginal gloss on fol. 82 R of Codex 875 of Reims. This is probably the hand of Eriugena. Ludwig Traube, who made this identification, describes this hand as follows: "The characteristic hand of an Irish scholar. It does not run across the vellum but dwells pensively and emphatically, yet without reserve, on words and sentences. Eriugena uses abbreviations sparingly; sometimes he invents an abbreviation, but one that is easily understood."

Among later works which are ascribed to John Scottus in manuscripts or can be claimed for him with good reason I mention a commentary on the theological treatises of Boethius, a brief Vita of this philosopher, a commentary on the Gospel of St. John, and a homily on the prologue to this Gospel. His commentary on the *Celestial Hierarchy* of Pseudo-Dionysius has already been mentioned.

John Scottus also wrote a number of poems, some in Latin, some in Greek, and some in a mixture of both. They are interesting to us because they yield information concerning his personal religion and his relations to the court. Those in Latin give proof of formal competence, which in his time had come to be taken for granted; those in Greek are remarkable by the very fact of their existence. Unlike Sedulius Scottus, however, John was no genuine poet.

About the last years of John's life we know as little as we know about his youth. There is no trace of him after 870. William of Malmesbury, who wrote in the early twelfth century, tells us that John Scottus, having become suspect of heresy in France, betook himself to the court of Alfred the Great of England and later taught at Malmesbury. There his students are said to have murdered him with their metal styluses, "because he forced them to think". Similar stories about teachers punished or murdered by their pupils are known from pagan and Christian antiquity. The alleged motive of Eriugena's students, even if the story is legendary, gives evidence of a deep knowledge of human nature.

Before taking leave of Eriugena, I should like to quote one other passage from his major work, because it testifies to Ireland's influence in a field of which little mention has so far been made—that of music. The music of antiquity and of the ancient Church knew neither harmony nor polyphony; it was essentially of the kind that is known to us from plain chant. By the term "harmony" the ancients understood the regular relation of one tone to another within a definite system, and not the simultaneous sounding of several notes forming a chord. Polyphony originated in the north and north-west of Europe. Its most primitive form was probably the *baritus* or *barditus* of the ancient Germans, that terrifying battle-cry of which Tacitus and other ancient writers make mention. In the literature on musical theory, the earliest treatise on polyphony is, in all probability, the so-called *Musica Enchiriadis*. It is found in numerous manuscripts, and under the names of several different authors. John Scottus, in the third book of his *Periphyseon*, illustrates the meaning and function of contraries in created nature by a comparison taken from music, which describes a similar form of polyphony as that of the *Musica Enchiriadis* (iii. 6):

For as instrumental music is composed of notes of different length and quality (pitch), which, heard in isolation, differ considerably according to tension, but if they are combined variously in certain relations according to the rules of musical theory result in sounds of a natural sweetness, so also the unity of the universe is made up of the parts, dissonant from one another when considered separately, yet of one all-embracing nature.

John Scottus on
Harmony.
MS Bamberg
Ph 2 1 fol. 151 R.

The impression that John Scottus is thinking of a type of music which he knew from his native country is confirmed by a comparison of this passage with the description of Irish musicians and their art by Giraldus Cambrensis (iii. 13):

It is only in the case of musical instruments that I find any commendable diligence in this people. They seem to me to be incomparably more skilled in these than any other people that I have seen. The movement is not, as in the British instrument to which we are accustomed, slow and easy, but rather quick and lively, while at the same time the melody is sweet and pleasant. It is remarkable how in spite of the great speed of the fingers, the musical proportion is maintained. The melody is kept perfect and full with unimpaired art through everything —through quivering measures and the involved use of several instruments—with a rapidity that charms, a rhythmic pattern that is varied, and a concord achieved through elements discordant. They harmonize at intervals of the octave and the fifth, but they always begin with B flat and with B flat end, so that everything may be rounded with the sweetness of charming sonority. They glide so subtly from one mode to another, and the grace notes so freely sport with such abandon and bewitching charm around the steady tone of the heavier sound, that the perfection of their art seems to lie in their concealing it, as if " it were the better for being hidden. An art revealed brings shame." Hence it happens that the very things that afford unspeakable delight to the minds of those who have a fine perception and can penetrate carefully to the secrets of the art, bore, rather than delight, those who have no such perception—who look without seeing, and hear without being able to understand. When the audience is unsympathetic they succeed only in causing boredom with what appears to be but confused and disordered noise.

In the opinion of Jacques Handschin, a leading historian of music of the last generation, the *Musica Enchiriadis* is the work of an Irishman. This theory is steadily gaining ground. It matters little whether

Eriugena actually knew this work either in Ireland or on the Continent or merely describes from his own experience a musical practice the theory of which is explained in the treatise. The conjecture that Ireland might have given polyphony to the Middle Ages is confirmed indirectly by the fact that just at the time when Saint Gall came under strong Irish influence this monastery began to take the lead in the development of music.

THE BOOK OF KELLS   The mutual character of the new relations between Ireland and the Continent is seen also in the art of that period. For the first time for centuries the country where Irish influence was strongest had developed an artistic style of its own, eclectic though it was, which invited imitation. Some of the canon tables of the Book of Kells (down to folio 4V) are probably modelled on those of an early Carolingian manuscript of the so-called Ada group. Comparison with the Leningrad Bede, a manuscript which was written in either Wearmouth or Jarrow, reveals strikingly the close links of the "Kells" artists with those of Northumbria. It has been suggested that the Book of Kells was written in Iona, and that it was taken to Kells for safety before the Viking raid of 806. This conjecture, plausible as it is, cannot be proved, but it is safe to say that the manuscript was written either late in the eighth century or about the year 800. It represents Irish calligraphy and illumination in its full maturity, and as far as we know is the most richly decorated manuscript ever produced by an Irish scriptorium. In addition to the standard decoration of manuscripts of its class it contains several pages of ornamental script, emphasizing important passages of the sacred text, and several full-page illuminations—the temptation of Christ, the arrest of Christ, the Virgin and Child—which are not known from other surviving manuscripts of this type. Hardly a single page of this book is without ornament of some sort. Characteristic are initials which blossom out into plant or animal motifs; the same, on a smaller scale, is true of many letters within the text.

On the Continent the expansion of Irish and Anglo-Saxon minuscule was checked by the development of Carolingian calligraphy, which reached a high degree of perfection first in the productions of the palace school, then, after Alcuin's death, in the scriptorium of Tours, and later in a number of other scriptoria, where we encounter characteristic variations of the basic type. This script, with its clear and graceful lettering, its regularity and legibility, was equally suitable for liturgical manuscripts and for school books. Alcuin had also revived the capital scripts of classical Rome, which provided several "display alphabets". These were soon graded in a "hierarchical" order, which is best known from the great Bibles of the school of Tours. The titles of Biblical books are normally in *Capitalis quadrata*, the text opens with a large initial which often combines insular and continental ornament, and alongside this initial the text is written in scripts which become less and less "display"—from *capitalis* over uncial and half-uncial down to minuscule. Tours produced a very stylized half-uncial of its own, which is used also for prefaces (including the *Novum opus* prologue of the Gospels) and for the introductions to individual Biblical books. *Capitalis rustica* is used frequently also for column titles and colophons. Irishmen would still use the script which they had learnt at home, as apparently did John Scottus—if, as has been suggested, the marginal glosses of some manuscripts now at Laon, Reims, and Bamberg are in his own hand. By and large, however, the influence of the Irish script became restricted to "symptoms" or traces in the hands of Carolingian scribes, and even these are rare in the masterpieces of the great writing centres.

Ornamentation, on the other hand, continued to be dominated considerably by the insular style. Even there, however, a new artistic feeling is unmistakable. The exuberance of the Irish imagination is reduced to a limited number of regular types. This change is very much in evidence in the ninth-century initials of the school of Saint Gall. The same tendency is manifest in the ornamentation of that

Detail from the initial X in the Christ-monogram on fol. 34 R of the Book of Kells.

de luxe style which Delisle termed "franco-saxon" and which we now, more cautiously, call franco-insular. It is seen in a considerable number of manuscripts of splendid execution, originating from northern France and Belgium, which are written in Carolingian minuscule and illuminated in a style which takes its ornamental motifs, interlacing bands and stylized animals, from insular art but treats them in a schematic, not to say pedantic manner. Famous specimens of this type are the Gospels of Saint Vaast at Arras, the Liège Sacramentary, now at Vienna (National Library, Codex 958), both from the middle of the ninth century, and the "Second Bible of Charles the Bald" (Paris, Bibliothèque Nationale, ms. lat. 2) of 865. Although the motifs of ornamentation are almost all derived from insular models, the general impression of franco-insular illumination is quite different. Most striking is perhaps its different colour scheme: the lavish use of gold and silver tincture, in particular, is as characteristic of Carolingian illumination as it is alien to that of England and Ireland. The same colours are employed for the ornamental script of specially elaborate pages, which are written in that ornamental alphabet which we have encountered in the Books of Kells and Lindisfarne. For about half a century this style was very fashionable; one of its leading scriptoria apparently was Saint-Amand near Valenciennes, under the abbots Milo and Hucbald.

In ninth-century Ireland a new type of high cross began to appear. On the surfaces of these crosses Biblical scenes in relief occupy more and more space at the expense of other ornamentation. This style is fully developed in the tenth century, especially in the north. Muiredach's cross at Monasterboice is fairly accurately dated by the abbot's obit in 923. This massive stone cross, about eighteen feet high, presents in the centre on one side the Crucifixion, on the other the Last Judgement; the front and back of its shaft are divided into panels with scenes from the Old and New Testament, while the other two sides are lavishly ornamented. The structure and grouping of these Biblical scenes is interpreted by Liam and Máire de Paor as an anticipation of romanesque art.

From the beginning of the tenth century, too, date the earliest round towers. These towers, by which the Irish landscape is dominated to the present day, must be understood as a specifically Irish version of an early Italian type of campanile. They taper off towards the top and are covered by a conical roof. That they, like their Italian models, were originally bell-towers is confirmed by their Irish name: *cloicthech*, "bell-house". In times of danger, however, they were used also as watch-towers and places of refuge. They have no entrance on ground level and can be entered only with the help of a ladder—which, in the face of danger, was hauled into the tower by the last of its temporary occupants. Whereas the churches and libraries of Irish monasteries fell victims to the plundering strangers, the high crosses and round towers, manifestations of the nation's will to survive, have out-lived all the storms of Irish history.

EPILOGUE

F after the end of the ninth century the Irish were no longer the leaven of intellectual life in continental Europe, the reason is to be sought in the decline of monastic learning in their own country. This decline resulted as much from the growing secular spirit within the monasteries as from the destruction wrought by the Vikings. Numerous Irish pilgrims would still travel on the Continent in order to visit Rome, or the holy places in Palestine, or the shrines of their own countrymen in Italy, Germany, and France. Such pilgrimages were particularly frequent during the eleventh century. We know of many Irish kings and ecclesiastical dignitaries who went on pilgrimage, but there must have been many more pilgrims who have remained unknown. An Irish pilgrim named Colmán (Kolomann), passing through Austria on his way to the Holy Land, was mistaken for a spy and murdered near Stockerau in 1012. The murdered stranger, however, proved his sanctity by miracles. The Emperor Henry II had his body solemnly transferred to Melk on the Danube, and Kolomann became one of the patrons of Austria.

If Irishmen settled on the Continent, which even then was not unheard of, they usually went further east—along and even across the Rhine, where, earlier than in France, the declining Carolingians had given place to a new and vigorous dynasty, the Saxon kings. Irishmen in Lorraine played some role, though not a leading one, in the ecclesiastical reforms which centred on Metz, Verdun, and Gorze-Trèves. An Irish bishop named Iohannes preached among the heathen in northern Germany and died there as a martyr about the year 1066. Hand in hand with the reform of Gorze-Trèves the cult and legend of Irish saints spread further in Germany. During the tenth century the legend of St. Brendan was brought to Trèves—possibly by a refugee bishop, Israel Brittigena or Scottigena—and from there to Ratisbon. Bishop Israel, it would seem, gave the *Voyage of St. Brendan* the literary form in which this story conquered the Middle Ages. The cult of this saint (whose name took the form Brandan in the German-speaking area) travelled all along the Baltic coast and (as Carl Selmer plausibly suggests) gave Brandenburg its name. Bishop Israel was the teacher of Bruno, the future archbishop of Cologne (d. 965). For some time the Rhine valley was the centre of dissemination of Hiberno-Latin literature on the Continent; by this road the legend of St. Patrick reached south-eastern Germany.

There is good evidence of the fact that during the tenth century the cult of Irish saints struck deep roots in France, Germany, and Italy. More and more Irish saints are represented in the collections of *Vitae Sanctorum*. The eleventh and twelfth centuries may be regarded as the classical age of the large *Legendarium* or *Passionale per Circulum Anni*—collections of hagiographical texts, often in a series of folio volumes, arranged in the order of the ecclesiastical calendar. This type of Legendarium is found first in France, later also in Germany and England. Its Italian counterpart is the combined Passional and Homiliary, which provides matter for public reading on all the Sundays and feasts of the ecclesiastical year—Lives of the saints on their feast-days, sermons for all the other occasions. A group of such manuscripts in Beneventan script of the eleventh century, which contain Cogitosus's Life of St. Brigit, bear witness to her cult in southern Italy; the metrical *Vita* of this saint, presumably a work of Donatus of Fiesole, is known only from Italian manuscripts of this time. This evidence links up with a note in a Vatican manuscript (Lat. 378), which refers to a group of Irish monks at Santa Maria in Palladio, Rome, towards the end of the eleventh century.

About this time a new Irish wave reached Central Europe: the "Schottenklöster". An Irish monk and scribe named Marianus (his full Irish name was Muiredach mac Robartaigh), a native of Donegal and member of the O'Donnel family, those hereditary custodians of the *Cathach* of St. Columcille, went on a pilgrimage to Rome with two companions in 1067. Passing through Germany, the pilgrims stayed for one year on the Michaelsberg near Bamberg. They stopped again at Ratisbon, and were invited to stay. They were given a church outside the city, Weih-Sankt-Peter, and settled down beside it, in single cells as was their native custom, in 1070. Marianus lived there as head of a small community until his death in 1080. Two manuscripts from his pen have survived: a copy of the Pauline Epistles with glosses, partly in Irish, which are indebted to Pelagius (now Vienna, Codex 1247), and another codex which after the dissolution of the Ratisbon "Schottenkloster" was taken to Fort Augustus in Scotland; the text of the latter breaks off in the middle of a sentence—Marianus died over his work. One generation after his death monks from Weih-Sankt-Peter founded the monastery of St. James, Ratisbon. They now lived a communal life under one roof and adopted the Benedictine Rule; Weih-Sankt-Peter was henceforth a priory under the jurisdiction of the abbot of St. James's. This was the first of those Irish Benedictine monasteries which came to be known as "Schottenklöster".

From Ratisbon, the Irish monastery near Würzburg was founded in 1135. Duke Henry of Austria, by-named Jasomirgott, called Irish monks ("Schottenmönche") to Vienna in 1155; the Vienna Schottenkloster still exists as a Benedictine monastery with a famous Gymnasium. New foundations followed: at Nuremberg, Erfurt, Konstanz, Eichstätt, and elsewhere. Two of Marianus's monks went as far as Russia in order to found a monastery at Kiev, to whose prince one of them was to bear a message from the Emperor, Henry IV. However, the plan miscarried. The two monks returned, with a present of valuable hides which largely paid for the building of St. James's Church at Ratisbon. Kiev had its Schottenkloster later, from the end of the twelfth century to the Mongol invasion of 1241; its monks came for the greater part from Vienna.

These new Irish monasteries soon received substantial donations and were able to procure numerous privileges, in particular exemption from all secular jurisdiction except the Emperor's, and from all ecclesiastical jurisdiction except that of the Holy See. It is thus not surprising that there were frequent conflicts with the local bishops, and the Irish, as one might expect, never failed to rise to the occasion. They must have come in for much criticism. One answer to their critics was probably the "Schotten-legende", which was launched from Ratisbon in the thirteenth century; this legend claims that the Schottenkloster at Ratisbon was founded by no less a person than Charlemagne.

Throughout the twelfth century and later, Ratisbon maintained close relations with Ireland. Abbots of St. James's visited their native country at regular intervals in order to recruit novices and to look after the two Irish priories under their jurisdiction. Abbot Christian MacCarthy, a relative of King Cormac MacCarthy of Munster, died at Cashel during such a visit in 1150. Whether the northern façade of the church of St. James at Ratisbon testifies to a continued tradition of Irish art in Germany is a disputed problem in the history of art. There can be no doubt, however, that the church which King Cormac erected on the rock of Cashel ("Cormac's Chapel", completed in 1134) owes something to the German romanesque style. At Ratisbon a monk named Marcus wrote the famous *Vision of Tundalus*, the account of a vision which one of the knights of Cormac of Cashel, Tundalus, was said to have had at Cork in 1148. It belongs to a group of writings which were produced in the interest of the new reform movement within the Irish Church, of which we shall hear shortly. The author, who shows himself to be very well acquainted with Irish ecclesiastical affairs, introduces in this vision of the other world meetings between Tundalus and a number of recently deceased persons who had played some part in that reform. In general outline the *Vision of Tundalus* follows the established forms of vision literature known from such works as the *Visions of St. Fursa* or the *Vision of Adamnán*. Ratisbon

was probably also the last link in the transmission of numerous Lives of Irish saints which, some time after 1181, were incorporated in the *Magnum Legendarium Austriacum.*

For centuries the "Schottenklöster" remained Irish in character. Towards the end of the Middle Ages, when the recruiting of novices in Ireland proved increasingly difficult, they were taken over by German Benedictines. They had probably slackened in religious fervour and monastic discipline as had monasteries generally in the decline of the Middle Ages, but there is some reason for doubting that they were as much worse than other religious as their successors tended to make them out.

Processional cross from Abyssinia. The combination of symbolical and purely geometrical ornament is perhaps an analogy with early Irish art. British Museum.

Once more we must turn to the Irish at home, and see how the Irish Church was affected by these renewed contacts with the Continent.

After the expulsion of the Vikings the ancient monasteries were rebuilt and the traditional organization of the Church was restored. Monastic life, however, was never again what it once had been; not even the Culdees differed greatly from the rest. In the margin of a schoolbook which was written at Glendalough about the year 1100 a note in Irish says: "This is the eve of Lugnasad (August 1st). I have a terrible headache." August 1st was a quarter day and was apparently celebrated. On the other hand we learn from the two scholastic fragments from Glendalough—the one contains the introduction to the grammar of Clemens, the other a text *De Abaco* which suggests a connexion with Chartres—and from the John Scottus extracts in an Irish manuscript of the twelfth century not only

Opposite:
The Processional
Cross of Cong. 11th
century.
National Museum,
Dublin.

that the study of the *Artes* had been resumed in Ireland but that scholars took an interest in the work of their compatriots on the Continent and in the new teaching that was on its way in the European schools.

More remarkable is the renaissance of national literature which followed upon the victory at Clontarf. The ancient sagas and genealogies of noble families were collected, chronicles were compiled, learned poetry flourished, and the great literary themes of antiquity were treated in Irish. Ecclesiastical and secular culture were brought closer to each other. A good example of this *rapprochement* is the Book of the Dun Cow (so called after the brown cow-hide of its binding), which contains, besides the earliest surviving texts of some Irish sagas, ecclesiastical literature such as the *Vision of Adamnán* and the *Sex Aetates Mundi*. The manuscript was written at Clonmacnoise about the year 1106.

The ecclesiastical situation had changed in so far as the remaining Scandinavian population in the seaports—in Dublin, Limerick, Waterford, Wexford—had accepted Christianity and gradually coalesced with native Irish society. It is perhaps not accidental that these cities were the first centres of regular dioceses, that their bishops were consecrated at Canterbury and professed obedience to the archbishops of England's primatial see, such as Lanfranc or Anselm. A bishop of Limerick, Gilla (Gillebert) Easpuic, who exchanged letters with St. Anselm in 1107, was the first to exhort the Irish clergy in an open letter to bring about a reform of the Irish Church in the double sense of a renewal of genuine religious life and of conforming with Rome in matters of liturgy and church organization. As in the seventh century, the reform had its most fervent supporters in the south. Among them was the king of Munster, Muirchertach Ua Briain, who in 1101 had made over to the Church the ancestral seat of the Munster kings, the Rock of Cashel. He also attended a synod convened by Gillebert at Rath Bresail in 1110. At this synod Ireland was divided into twenty-four dioceses under two metropolitans, the archbishops of Cashel and Armagh.

The ancient monasteries showed little inclination to accept the new order. Their opposition was all the stronger for the fact that in many places lay abbots, chosen from the local dynasties and noble families according to secular hereditary law, wielded all the real power and treated priests and bishops as their subordinates. The conflict between tradition and reform is best known at Armagh, because we still possess the Life of the reformer in this province, Archbishop Malachy, written by his friend, St. Bernard of Clairvaux. At Armagh eight successive members of the Ui Sinaich family had ruled as lay abbots. The last of these, however, Cellach, who by the right of family succession had become abbot in 1105, was won over to reform. He took holy orders and was consecrated archbishop of Armagh at Cashel in the following year. As his successor he had earmarked a young priest named Máel-Máedóc (latinized Malachias), whom he had sent for training to Malchus of Lismore, a champion of the reform. After Cellach's death (1129), however, the Ui Sinaich family appointed first Muirchertach, a son of Cellach's predecessor, and after his death (1134) a brother of Cellach as *comarba*. Malachy had to fight hard for his right against these lay pretenders. He did his best to introduce in the north the reforms of Rath Bresail. In 1139 he went to Rome in order to obtain from Pope Innocent II the pallia for the two Irish archbishops. By this time he had already resigned the archbishopric and had retired to Bangor. The Pope demanded that the pallia should be asked for at an Irish synod, but made Malachy his legate in Ireland. On his way to and from Rome Malachy stayed at Clairvaux. He was full of admiration for the strict life of the Cistercians and entered into an intimate friendship with St. Bernard, whose advice and support he enjoyed in taking one of the most decisive steps in the ecclesiastical history of Ireland. He left four of his companions at Clairvaux to be trained in the Cistercian way of life. With these and some monks of Clairvaux he founded the first Irish Cistercian abbey, Mellifont near Drogheda, in 1142. The magnificent buildings, which are impressive even as ruins, were not completed until 1157, nine years after Malachy's death, nor did he live to attend the national synod which he had prepared. It was held at Kells in 1152. At this synod the reform of the Irish Church was completed. The number of archbishops was raised to four (Armagh, Cashel, Tuam, and Dublin), and they were given their pallia. The Irish Church had thus become in every respect a regular part of the Western Church. When in 1169 the deposed king of Leinster, Diarmait mac Murchada, called in the Anglo-Normans in the hope of recovering the throne with their help, and these turned their aid into a conquest of Ireland, there was very little still in need of reform. The conquerors were content with making the Church of Ireland dependent on the Church of England, and with putting Englishmen in all higher places of ecclesiastical office as far as their power extended. The *Hibernenses* or *Hibernici* of later medieval literature—Petrus Hibernicus, a teacher of St. Thomas, or Thomas Hibernicus, a professor of the Sorbonne (d. 1316)—were Anglo-Irish. The *doctor subtilis*, Duns Scotus, was not Irish but Scottish.

If during the later Middle Ages the Irish more or less fade out of the intellectual life of Europe, the Irish heritage was preserved. In the Latin script the insular system of abbreviation was combined with the continental one as early as the eleventh century; in this form it continued to be in use far beyond the Middle Ages. The Irish principle of articulating a text by initials of different size and elaboration was also taken over and further developed. The Irish saints were invoked as before. Their feasts are found in many a late medieval calendar. Their legends were re-copied and, in abridged form, inserted in numerous breviaries as the historical lessons for their respective days; many of them reached innumerable readers through the *Golden Legend* of Iacobus a Voragine of Genoa (d. 1298). The popularity of Irish saints during the later Middle Ages can be measured by the great number of Guilds and religious brotherhoods who made them their patrons. The "Purgatory of St. Patrick" on an island of Lough Derg in Donegal, in the hands of Augustinians since the twelfth century, was one of the most famous places of pilgrimage of medieval Europe, where many a famous or infamous nobleman professed to have had visions of the other world. On the report of a disillusioned pilgrim Pope Alexander VI ordered the Purgatory to be closed, but he had little success; the pilgrimage continued, even in penal times, and (in a mitigated form) is still the most popular in Ireland. The visions of a knight, Sir Owain, during the reign of King Stephen of England (1135–54) in that place of penance were described in great detail by a monk of Saltrey. This text, together with the *Vision of Tundalus* and the *Voyage of St. Brendan*, was one of the most read books of the late Middle Ages. Not only was the original Latin text frequently copied, it was also translated into most of the medieval vernaculars.

The theology, the classical learning, and the scientific knowledge of Ireland's golden age were left behind by the progress made in later times. They were forgotten until modern historians began to study them. As a result of these studies we may say without exaggeration not only that works of lasting value were produced by some outstanding Irish scholars, but also that Irish learning gave the nascent Middle Ages a stimulus which enabled them to outgrow their masters.

Irish art, on the other hand, can claim a place in European civilization entirely on its own merit. This art, whether it is manifested in metal and stone or on the illuminated pages of manuscripts over the wide field of Irish expansion from Scotland to Franconia and Italy, is not only unique in the Middle Ages, it is also the first, and in the West the only, example of an abstract art in an articulate civilization which was still spiritually integrated. Even if it did not survive as a distinct entity outside its country of origin, it was at least one of the determining factors that shaped Carolingian art, and its spirit can still be felt in the romanesque art of the eleventh and twelfth centuries. Gothic art broke away from this path and took a new direction. We at present stand at the end of the way which the art of Europe has since taken. Our eyes are opened again for the appreciation of Irish art, which is one of the glories of our Western heritage.

NOTE

On the poem on pages 59-61

   This poem is cast in dialogue form. In the opening stanza (preceding the first printed here) Gúaire, the seventh-century king of Connacht, questions the hermit Marbán as to why he leads a life lacking all normal comfort. Then the hermit expounds his way of life and its delights. The poem concludes with a single stanza spoken by the king:

> My power of kingship I will give,
> my father Colmán's heritage,
> and full possession until my death,
> to be with you there, O Marbán.

   The poem is generally regarded as belonging to the ninth century. To the present writer, however, it appears that what we have here is in fact two ninth-century poems, probably from a saga, loosely joined together in a slightly later dialogue framework. The poems are spoken by a hermit of the type of Mad Sweeney, Myrddin, or Merlin, who are, of course, all closely related characters. Marbán's bothy is not a real bothy but, like Mad Sweeney's, made by God. It is on a great height and is to be compared with Merlin's dwelling as described by Geoffrey of Monmouth in his *Vita Merlini*:

> *Fons erat in summo cuiusdam vertice montis*
> *Undique precinctus corulis densaque frutectis*
> *Illic Merlinus consederat.*

   In the second poem there are a number of difficulties, mainly of a botanical nature. In this matter, and in certain others, I have followed the suggestions of Gerard Murphy, to whose edition and translation (*Early Irish Lyrics*, p. 10 ff.) I am much indebted. As Professor Bieler points out to me, *densaque* in the Vita Merlini is both ungrammatical and unmetrical; it should probably be changed to *densusque*.

J. C.

SOURCES

ST. PATRICK, *Confessio; Epistola:* L. Bieler, *Libri Epistolarum S. Patricii Episcopi,* 2 vols. (Dublin, 1952).

COGITOSUS: Cogitosus, *Vita S. Brigidae,* in *Acta Sanctorum,* February 11 (1658), pp. 135–141.

COLUMBANUS: *S. Columbani Opera,* ed. G. S. M. Walker, Scriptores Latini Hiberniae, vol. 2 (Dublin, 1957).

ADAMNAN: William Reeves, *The Life of St. Columba, Founder of Hy, written by Adamnán* (Dublin, 1857). *Adamnán's Life of Columba,* ed. A. O. and M. O. Anderson (London, 1961).

PENITENTIALIS VINNIANI and DE ARREIS: L. Bieler and D. A. Binchy, *The Irish Penitentials,* Scriptores Latini Hiberniae, vol. 5.

MURPHY, G., *Early Irish Lyrics* (Oxford, 1956).

ANTIPHONARY OF BANGOR: F. E. Warren, *The Antiphonary of Bangor,* 2 vols. (London 1893, 1895). (Henry Bradshaw Society, vols. 4 & 10.)

BEDE: Charles Plummer, *Bede: The Historical Works,* 2 vols. (Oxford, 1896).

EKKEHARD IV: *Monumenta Germaniae Historica,* Scriptores, vol. 2, pp. 74–147.

VITA S. RICHARII: *Monumenta Germaniae Historica,* Scriptores Rerum Merovingicarum, vol. 7, pp. 438–453.

VITA S. FURSEI, ADDITAMENTUM NIVIALENSE DE S. FUILANO: *Monumenta Germaniae Historica,* Scriptores Rerum Merovingicarum, vol. 4.

TRAUBE, L., *Peronna Scottorum,* in Sitzungsberichte München, 1900.

DÜMMLER, E., *Monumenta Germaniae Historica,* Epistulae, vol. 3 (1891), p. 360 (Pope Zacharias to Boniface).

GIRALDUS: John J. O'Meara, "Giraldus Cambrensis in Topographia Hiberniae", in *Proceedings of the Royal Irish Academy,* 52 C 4, 1949.

GESTA KAROLI MAGNI: ed. H. F. Haefele (Berlin 1959).

JOHANNES SCOTTUS: Migne, *Patrologiae Cursus Completus,* Series Latina, vol. 122.

DICUIL: G. Parthey, *Dicuili Liber de Mensura Orbis Terrae* (Berlin, 1870).

SEDULIUS SCOTTUS: *Monumenta Germaniae Historica,* Poetae, vol. 3, 1886.

The following English translations have been used:

ST. PATRICK: *The Works of St. Patrick,* trans. L. Bieler, Ancient Christian Writers, vol. 17 (Westminster, Md., Newman Press, London, Longmans Green, 1953).

ST. COLUMBANUS: *S. Columbani Opera,* ed. G. S. M. Walker (Dublin, Institute for Advanced Studies, 1957).

ADAMNAN: *Life of St. Columba,* ed. A. O. and M. O. Anderson (London, Nelsons, 1961).

BEDE: *Historical Works,* trans. J. E. King, Loeb Classical Library (London, Heinemann, 1954).

GIRALDUS CAMBRENSIS: *Topography of Ireland,* trans. J. J. O'Meara (Dundalk, Dundalgan Press, 1951).

VINNIAN; COMMUTATIONS: trans. L. Bieler and D. A. Binchy (Dublin, Institute for Advanced Studies, 1963).

All other prose translations were made by the author specially for this book.

LIST OF ILLUSTRATIONS

The coloured reproductions are marked with an asterisk